INFECTIOUS FUNGI

Anthrax

Avian Flu

Botulism

Campylobacteriosis

Cholera

Ebola

Encephalitis

Escherichia coli Infections

Gonorrhea

Hantavirus Pulmonary Syndrome

Hepatitis

Herpes

HIV/AIDS

Infectious Fungi

Influenza

Legionnaires' Disease

Leprosy

Lyme Disease

Mad Cow Disease (Bovine Spongiform Encephalopathy)

Malaria

Meningitis

Mononucleosis

Pelvic Inflammatory Disease

Plague

Polio

Salmonella

SARS

Smallpox

Streptococcus (Group A)

Staphylococcus aureus Infections

Syphilis

Toxic Shock Syndrome

Tuberculosis

Tularemia

Typhoid Fever

West Nile Virus

DEADLY DISEASES AND EPIDEMICS

INFECTIOUS FUNGI

David L. Brock

FOUNDING EDITOR
The Late **I. Edward Alcamo**
Distinguished Teaching Professor of Microbiology,
SUNY Farmingdale

FOREWORD BY
David Heymann
World Health Organization

CHELSEA HOUSE
P U B L I S H E R S
An imprint of Infobase Publishing

Infectious Fungi

Chelsea House
An imprint of Infobase Publishing
132 West 31st Street
New York NY 10001

Library of Congress Cataloging-in-Publication Data

Brock, David L., 1963–
   Infectious fungi/David L. Brock.
      p. cm.—(Deadly diseases and epidemics)
    ISBN 0-7910-8680-1
   1. Mycoses—Juvenile literature. I. Title. II. Series.
RC117.B76 2005
616.9'69—dc22   2005021151

Chelsea House books are available at special discounts when purchased in bulk quantities for businesses, associations, institutions, or sales promotions. Please call our Special Sales Department in New York at (212) 967-8800 or (800) 322-8755.

You can find Chelsea House on the World Wide Web at http://www.chelseahouse.com

Text design by Terry Mallon
Cover design by Keith Trego

Printed in the United States of America

Bang 21C 10 9 8 7 6 5 4 3 2 1

This book is printed on acid-free paper.

All links and web addresses were checked and verified to be correct at the time of publication. Because of the dynamic nature of the web, some addresses and links may have changed since publication and may no longer be valid.

Table of Contents

Foreword

In the 1960s, many of the infectious diseases that had terrorized generations were tamed. After a century of advances, the leading killers of Americans both young and old were being prevented with new vaccines or cured with new medicines. The risk of death from pneumonia, tuberculosis (TB), meningitis, influenza, whooping cough, and diphtheria declined dramatically. New vaccines lifted the fear that summer would bring polio, and a global campaign was on the verge of eradicating smallpox worldwide. New pesticides like DDT cleared mosquitoes from homes and fields, thus reducing the incidence of malaria, which was present in the southern United States and which remains a leading killer of children worldwide. New technologies produced safe drinking water and removed the risk of cholera and other water-borne diseases. Science seemed unstoppable. Disease seemed destined to all but disappear.

But the euphoria of the 1960s has evaporated.

The microbes fought back. Those causing diseases like TB and malaria evolved resistance to cheap and effective drugs. The mosquito developed the ability to defuse pesticides. New diseases emerged, including AIDS, Legionnaires, and Lyme disease. And diseases which had not been seen in decades re-emerged, as the hantavirus did in the Navajo Nation in 1993. Technology itself actually created new health risks. The global transportation network, for example, meant that diseases like West Nile virus could spread beyond isolated regions and quickly become global threats. Even modern public health protections sometimes failed, as they did in 1993 in Milwaukee, Wisconsin, resulting in 400,000 cases of the digestive system illness cryptosporidiosis. And, more recently, the threat from smallpox, a disease believed to be completely eradicated, has returned along with other potential bioterrorism weapons such as anthrax.

The lesson is that the fight against infectious diseases will never end.

In our constant struggle against disease, we as individuals have a weapon that does not require vaccines or drugs, and that is the warehouse of knowledge. We learn from the history of science that "modern" beliefs can be wrong. In this series of books, for example, you will learn that diseases like syphilis were once thought to be caused by eating potatoes. The invention of the microscope set science on the right path. There are more positive lessons from history. For example, smallpox was eliminated by vaccinating everyone who had come in contact with an infected person. This "ring" approach to smallpox control is still the preferred method for confronting an outbreak, should the disease be intentionally reintroduced.

At the same time, we are constantly adding new drugs, new vaccines, and new information to the warehouse. Recently, the entire human genome was decoded. So too was the genome of the parasite that causes malaria. Perhaps by looking at the microbe and the victim through the lens of genetics we will be able to discover new ways to fight malaria, which remains the leading killer of children in many countries.

Because of advances in our understanding of such diseases as AIDS, entire new classes of anti-retroviral drugs have been developed. But resistance to all these drugs has already been detected, so we know that AIDS drug development must continue.

Education, experimentation, and the discoveries that grow out of them are the best tools to protect health. Opening this book may put you on the path of discovery. I hope so, because new vaccines, new antibiotics, new technologies, and, most importantly, new scientists are needed now more than ever if we are to remain on the winning side of this struggle against microbes.

David Heymann
Executive Director
Communicable Diseases Section
World Health Organization
Geneva, Switzerland

1

What Is an Infectious Fungus?

Early one cold January morning, residents of Northridge, California slept quietly, unaware of the terrible force hurling toward them from dozens of miles inside the earth. When the quake hit at 4:31 A.M., most of them would only survive the next 15 seconds because of luck or a well built house, and many officials still consider it a miracle that only 51 people died.

While the 1994 Northridge earthquake injured thousands and caused billions of dollars in damage, what no one knew at the time was that it had also released a different potential killer, whose impact would last a lot longer than 15 seconds. The quake had stirred up the soil all over Ventura County and had propelled billions of spores of *Coccidioides immitis* into the air. **Valley Fever** had come to the Greater Los Angeles area, and by the time the three year **epidemic** was over, infections would rise from 400 to 4,500 patients per year and would cost more than $45 million in hospital and outpatient costs.

All because an earthquake set a **fungus** free.

FUNGI BASICS

But what is a fungus? Modern science classifies organisms according to features such as cell structure, means of acquiring energy, and reproductive methods. A fungus is an organism made up of **eukaryotic** cells that have a cell wall containing **chitin**. They are **heterotrophs** that are not capable of forming true **tissues** like more complex plants and animals, and they can reproduce both sexually and asexually. Biologists estimate that there are probably over 1.5 million species of fungi (though only about 100,000 have been identified). Traditionally, they classify fungi into three divisions according to differences in how they reproduce sexually: Zygomycota, Ascomycota, and Basidiomycota. Members of the Zygomycota division, for example, produce a unique, thick-walled covering that surrounds the fertilized cell, and a typical example of these fungi is bread mold. Ascomycota fungi on the other hand produce a saclike pouch which contains either four, but usually eight, fertilized cells. Fungi in this division that many people are familiar with are truffles. Finally, fungi classified as Basidiomycota reproduce using an enlarged, club-shaped structure that people typically call a mushroom. In fact, the actual organism we call a mushroom lives underground,

WORLD'S LARGEST ORGANISM?

Do you think the giant blue whale is the world's largest organism? Guess again! At a paltry 80 feet long and 100 tons, it doesn't even come close. How about the ancient redwood tree? With an average height of 240 feet, you would think nothing could be larger, but you'd still be wrong.

The world's largest organism is actually a fungus. Single individuals of certain soil fungi regularly grow to inhabit a dozen acres or more. They can penetrate the ground as deep as 10 feet down, and in Iron County Michigan, a fungus has been found that takes up 38 acres.

But the big winner so far is an *Armillaria ostoyae* found in Oregon that is 3.4 *miles* in diameter, weighs hundreds of tons, and is at least 2,400 years old. That's over 1,500 acres, and if you were to dig it up, it would occupy an area the size of downtown Washington, D.C.!

So the next time someone asks you what the largest thing alive is, you can look them in the eye and with confidence say, "why the common mushroom, of course."

and all that people see is the organ it uses to fertilize its reproductive cells.

While different species of fungi may reproduce sexually in different ways, any individual fungus will usually come in one of two physical forms. Either it will appear as unicellular yeast, or more commonly, it will exist as a multicellular mold. Molds consist of long, thin filaments called **hyphae** that allow the organism to spread out into its surrounding environment. These hyphae are usually between 3 and 10 mm in diameter but can be miles long. Each hypha is divided into individual cells by **septa** that allow for the exchange of materials through pores in them, and collectively, the hyphae serve as the means for all exchanges between the mold and its environment. Consequently, the type of hyphae directly reflects where a mold lives and what it does (Figure 1.1 for some examples of different hyphae).

Yeasts and molds reproduce in different ways. Yeast, for instance, will reproduce either by **mitosis**, or through a process called "**budding**." During mitosis, a yeast cell will duplicate its genetic material and divide into two new cells, each with a copy of the genetic instruction. In budding, the cell will create a bulge in its cell wall and membrane and protrude a new cell out of the original one (Figure 1.2). What distinguishes this process from regular cell division is that the protrusion remains part of the old cell. So as yeast buds, it will start to look like a string of pearls.

Molds, meanwhile, reproduce by creating and releasing **spores** in one of two ways. They can generate spores asexually through a process similar to budding. A hypha undergoes **mitosis** to make a new nucleus and then pinches off this nucleus into a new cell that can detach as a spore (unlike budding, the new cell is not still part of the original). Or they can generate spores sexually by uniting two nuclei and then dividing them and the cell through **meiosis** (Figure 1.3 for a diagram of what this looks like).

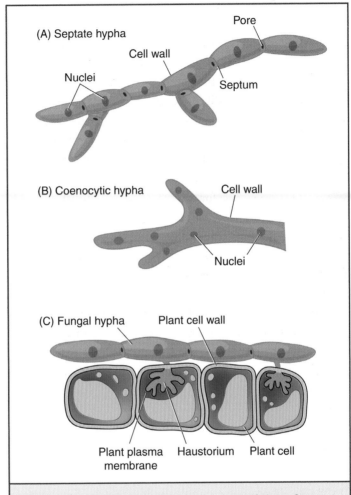

(A) Septate hypha

Pore

Cell wall

Nuclei

Septum

(B) Coenocytic hypha

Cell wall

Nuclei

(C) Fungal hypha

Plant cell wall

Plant plasma membrane

Haustorium

Plant cell

Figure 1.1 Hyphae usually come in one of three forms. (A) In septate hypha, a septa separates each cell of the fungus. (B) Coenocytic hypha contains few septae and has no real separation between cells. (C) Haustoria hypha has septae that separates individual cells, but has the ability to grow out finger-like projections to invade other organisms.

Regardless of whether a fungus is a yeast or a mold, however, it acquires its nutrients and energy the same basic way. All fungi release powerful enzymes that cause a process

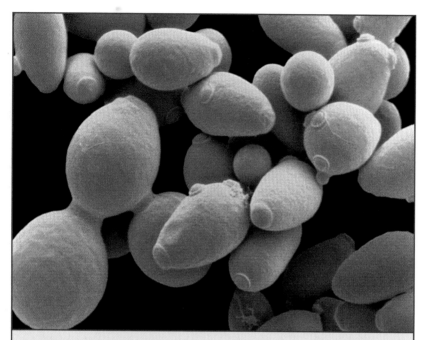

Figure 1.2 These yeast cells have started the budding process. The barbell-looking structures are yeast cells in the middle stage of their first protrusion. This photomicrograph was taken with a scanning electron microscope.

called **hydrolysis**. By adding water to large organic **polymers** such as proteins and carbohydrates, a fungus' hydrolytic enzymes break down the molecules of their food into simple **monomers**. The yeast or mold can then absorb them through its cell membrane and reassemble them into its own molecules. Human and other animals do the same basic thing with their digestive systems; fungi simply "digest" their food on the outside.

Because all fungi get their nutrition the same way, the vast majority of them are free living **saprobes** that decay dead organic matter. A few species are **parasitic,** digesting the surface of living organisms to harvest what they need, and some live in symbiotic harmony as part of the natural microscopic

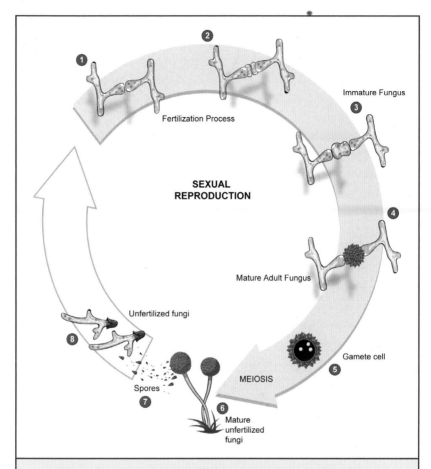

Figure 1.3 The typical reproductive cycle of a mold can occur either sexually (stages 1-8) or asexually. In stages 1 and 2, the unfertilized fungi unite, producing the cells from which adult fungus will grow (stage 3). In stage 4, the adult fungus releases a gamete cell which undergoes meiosis in stages 5 and 6, leading to unfertilized spores in stage 7. These spores then grow up into new unfertilized fungi (stage 8).

flora already inhabiting our bodies. But most are essentially scavengers, consuming what is already dead, and that is why so many of them, like the *C. immitis* involved in the Northridge epidemic, inhabit the soil.

INFECTIOUS FUNGI

With so many fungi—and so many living in the soil—why aren't there more outbreaks like the one in 1994? Furthermore, of the 100,000 known species of fungi, why are only 150 currently known to cause some kind of disease?

THE EARTH BENEATH OUR FEET

Until 400 million years ago, the earth was a rocky and barren place and almost all life was found under water. But then primitive plants began to move out of the seas, where their ancestors had lived for billions of years, and onto the land. With their arrival, the world as we know it began to evolve.

How did they do it? Well, it turns out we owe it all to fungi. The first creatures to colonize the land were **lichens**. These dual organisms (part fungus, part **algae**) worked together to break down rocks and other barren surfaces into the nutrients they needed to live. The fungus part would remove minerals the algae needed while the algae would use sunlight to make sugars for the fungus. A lichen could survive where nothing else could, but in the process, it also turned hard stone into soft soil—soil where the primitive plants could begin to take root.

But plants needed fungi for more than simply making soil. They also needed them to survive in it. The way it works today is that certain soil molds coil their long, thread-like hyphae around the roots of plants, forming **mycorrhizae**. Because the tiny fungi can go much deeper and into smaller spaces than a plant's roots can, the plant is able to get nutrients it otherwise couldn't. In turn, the plant provides more food than the fungi could ever absorb on their own. Thus, because of soil's fungi, plants can live on land—and so can all the *other* critters that depend on plants to survive. Fungi not only provide the dirt under our feet, but they also ultimately make it possible for all of us to be here on land in the first place.

The answer turns out to be that healthy humans have an extremely high level of natural immunity to most fungi. Intact skin and mucosal surfaces like those in the lungs and digestive tract prevent the majority of the pathogenic fungi from taking root, and with a working immune system, the odd fungus that does manage to attach to these surfaces will usually produce only a mild and self-limiting infection. In other words, even when a fungus does infect someone, their immune system can successfully fight off the infection without needing any active medical intervention. Any symptoms of the condition simply disappear after a while.

Where pathogenic fungi start to become a problem is in situations where the natural immune process no longer works the way it should. Patients with AIDS or cancer, for example, must watch their body's ability to protect itself ravaged as the HIV virus or chemotherapy destroy the very white blood cells needed for defense. Others such as transplant recipients must actually actively repress immunity to prevent organ rejection, and even people undergoing basic surgery place a strain on their immune system that opens them up to possible **secondary infection**.

The leading secondary infection in the **immunocompromised** today is a fungal infection. Fungi cause more **nosocomial** or hospital-acquired infections than any other type of **pathogen**. Researchers now know that over 40% of all deaths attributed to illnesses caught during a hospital stay have actually been the result of a fungus rather than a **bacterium** or **virus**.[1] Furthermore, this percentage continues to grow as the number of immunocompromised in our society, particularly the elderly, rises. Modern medical advances are keeping these individuals alive longer, and so the opportunity to catch a fungal infection steadily increases.

The rise in nosocomial deaths from catching a fungus, though, is not just because of an increase in the number of immunocompromised individuals. Simply diagnosing and treating fungal infections has proven quite difficult. Part of the problem is that unlike most pathogens, most fungi are free-living organisms; they do not need our bodies to reproduce. Hence, when doctors and other medical professionals first observe the usual flu-like symptoms or rash, they regularly attribute them to one of the organisms that usually do employ our bodies as **vectors** to reproduce (unlike fungi for whom we

FABULOUS FUNGI!

When you hear the word "fungus," what image pops into your head? The fuzz covered three-week old leftovers at the back of the fridge? A piece of cheddar cheese coated with blue and green splotches? Maybe an old news photo of slimy walls in a flood damaged house?

Whatever you recall, the odds are that first image won't be a good one. Most of our daily encounters with fungi seem to involve throwing out rotting food or listening to ads for cleaning products to fight mildew in our kitchens and bathrooms. Even the focus of this book is on fungi that can make us sick.

But the reality is that life without fungi would be pretty grim. Imagine a world of nothing but crackers because there isn't any yeast to make bread, or eating buffalo chicken wings without blue cheese dressing because there's no mold to make the main ingredient. In truth, without fungi, there would be no mushrooms or truffles to eat; no cola, beer, or wine to drink; no penicillin (or almost any other antibiotic) to fight infections...the list is *huge*. Fungi are a positive and integral part of almost every moment of our everyday lives. We literally can't live without them.

Nor would we want to; so the next time you eat a toasted bagel, fight off a week-old sore throat, or enjoy the tingling sensation of a glass of soda, remember that a fungus made it possible.

are simply hosts). Add in the fact that the severity of symptoms can vary dramatically depending on the site of the infection (even for the same species!), and the misdiagnosis of fungal disease is extremely common.

Doing so, of course, delays starting the correct treatment, and with fungi, correct treatment is critical. The reason is because most of the medicines we use to combat microbial infections are **antibiotics**, and while antibiotics successfully treat bacteria infections with few side-effects, they do so because bacteria are **prokaryotes**. Critical differences in cell structure between prokaryotes and **eukaryotes** like us cause antibiotics to kill bacteria without harming our body's own cells. But fungi are also eukaryotes; so giving a patient antibiotics will do the person no good (and as we shall see later in Chapter 8 can actually worsen the situation). Furthermore, because fungi are eukaryotes, almost any drug which kills them will kill or harm us as well. Thus, the number of medicines available to treat fungal infections is quite small and often species specific, making the correct treatment of a pathogenic fungus literally a potentially life and death matter.

Even with correct treatment, though, getting rid of an infectious fungus is not always easy. Many are becoming increasingly resistant to the medicines we do currently have. The organisms themselves are hard to grow in culture, making it difficult to develop new drugs (as well as adding to the challenge of diagnosis), and the list of possible pathogenic fungi keeps growing, each one regularly requiring its own unique drug with which to combat it.

But the real challenge behind eliminating an infectious fungus ultimately lies in how they cause illness in the first place. So let us turn to Chapter 2 to see how changes in the internal and external environment of the body can lead to a fungus' ability to colonize us.

2

Upsetting the Balance— How Fungi Make You Sick

Meet *Candida albicans*. **Like so many microbes,** this common, ordinary yeast is a natural part of the numerous **fauna** that call the human body home. They inhabit almost any warm, moist region, including the vagina, the mouth, and throughout most of the digestive tract. Under normal circumstances, members of this species live in balance with other inhabitants of our bodies such as *E. coli* and various other bacteria and **protists**. Together, they all form the natural microscopic ecosystem of the human body, and in a healthy body, we rarely notice they are even there.

But *C. albicans* is not always so **benign**. When changes occur in the body's internal environment (such as a decrease in acidity), the natural ecological balance gets thrown off. Then the body's yeasts can breed uninhibited. This growing population of yeast can get out of control, and the result is a yeast infection. The infection that develops depends on where the excess growth is taking place. The most common of them is **vulvovaginal candidiasis**, usually referred to as "a vaginal yeast infection" or simply "yeast infection." The other, far less frequent infections are **oropharyngeal candidiasis** or "**thrush**" and the even rarer invasive or systemic **candidemia**.

We will be looking at the clinical information about these three conditions in far more detail later in Chapter 3. But for now, the causal agent for them provides us with a model organism for how all fungi produce their variety of infections. What *C. albicans* does, the other infectious fungi basically do, too. So because this yeast is easy to culture (unlike many of the infectious fungi), making it easier to study, it provides an excellent window into the "*modus operandi*" for all the disease causing fungi.

BIOFILMS

There are essentially three key stages to all fungal infections. The first and most important of these is a change in the environment of the body. Before any fungus can invade, the normal **homeostasis** of the body has to break down. It can be something as simple as very damp feet or as complex as a diseased or damaged organ. But unless some environmental change upsets the chemical balance of the body, potential infectious fungi cannot find the nutritional resources they need to reproduce and multiply their numbers. This dependency on the status of the body's own ecology is a critical and unique feature of fungal diseases. Unlike most pathogens which have evolved active ways to breach the body's natural defenses, infectious fungi cannot invade without the body in some way aiding the process. Again, this "aid" may be as simple as the skin cells expending energy to cope with exposure to too much water or as complex as the immune system being preoccupied with cancer cells. But no matter what the fungal pathogen, the body's defensive "attention" must be out of balance before it can gain access to the metabolic resources it needs. Hence, whether the invading fungus is a non-opportunistic one such as the *Microsporum* mold that causes ringworm (see Chapter 4) or an opportunistic one such as *Aspergillis fumigatus* (see Chapter 6), it must have the body's "cooperation" in some fashion or another to do so.

Once a fungus has the body's "cooperation," it has access to its biochemical resources. It can then begin the second stage of infection which involves a simultaneous two-prong attack. As the fungus adheres to the tissue it is invading, it makes chemicals signals called prostaglandins that start to modify the body's immune system. The fungus suppresses or hides from the body's natural defenses just long enough for the adhering cells to start forming a **biofilm** at the site of the invasion. With the exception of only four fungal diseases we will discuss in Chapters 6 and 7, it is this biofilm that the body experiences as the actual infection. Hence, knowing how fungi create biofilms is critical to understanding how infectious fungi like *C. albicans* cause disease.

In general, a biofilm is a community of microbes that has colonized the surface of a structure by producing special chemicals. These chemicals glue the microbes both to each other and to the surface, allowing them to secure a safe, nourishing long-term habitat for themselves. Essentially, biofilm formation is to microbes what living in cities is to people. By banding together, the microbes are able to join resources to exploit the surrounding environment more effectively and to defend themselves better. It is why biofilms are such a nuisance and so problematic for medicine and industry. In the same way that it takes a lot of force, power, and resources to destroy a town or city completely because people can work together and help each other protect it, it takes potent drugs and chemicals applied often to kill off a biofilm for the same basic reason. This evolutionary advantage makes microbes which can form biofilms hardier, and modern medicine now acknowledges it is the typical method of growth and reproduction of fungi (and many bacteria) associated with infections.[1]

A biofilm starts to form whenever a few individual cells bump into a surface where they can attach. Specifically, some of the molecules on the surface must have shapes that match up with the shape of key proteins on the outside of the cells. These molecules and cell proteins must fit together exactly, like pieces in a puzzle (Figure 2.1). When they do, the cells forming the biofilm grab on and use the surface's molecules to hold themselves temporarily in place. This physical contact between the cells and the material activates certain genes. The cells use these genes to begin producing proteins called

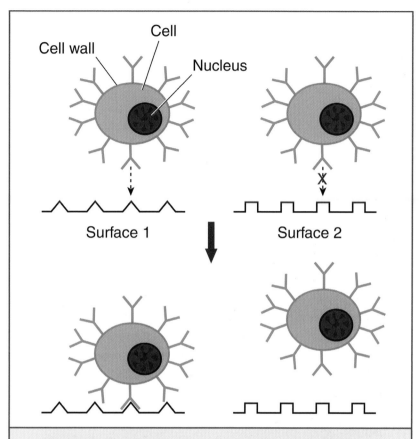

Figure 2.1 A cell's interaction with its environment depends on the shape of its external proteins. When the shapes match those found in its environment such as in surface 1, the cell can interact with it. If the shapes do not match, such as in surface 2, the cell cannot interact with it.

"**adhesins**," which enable them to attach themselves permanently to the surface. Next, the cells use the process of making adhesions to signal other genes that it is time to change which chemical reactions the cells perform. Essentially, the attached cells stop the **metabolic pathways** they use when they are floating around and free-living. Then, they start those pathways which will produce the chemicals they will need to survive bonded to the surface. In particular, they start to produce proteins for communication between the cells that will cause any neighboring cell or daughter cell to make molecules to fasten all the cells together. The result is that as the original cells reproduce and multiply, a giant scaffold of proteins forms. This scaffold interlocks all the cells together while the adhesins bind the entire colony permanently to the structure (Figure 2.2). The result is a slimy feeling "film" across its surface.

The basic mechanism for biofilm formation is fundamentally the same regardless of the type of microbe. Bacteria, algae, and fungi all use it to form films on a variety of both natural surfaces like the lining of the mouth and artificial surfaces like **catheters** and other medical implants. What makes fungi

THE COST OF DOING BUSINESS

Anyone who's ever owned a boat knows that the first thing you do when you take it out of the water is to hose it down. But did you ever know why? You might think it's just to clean it off. The real reason is that if you don't rinse off the bottom of your boat, a gooey layer of slime will start to form on it, and over time, that slime can lead to big trouble.

That slimy layer is really a biofilm. Left undisturbed, it will grow into an entire underwater "forest" of creatures, all living attached to your boat. Barnacles, clams, and mussels use biofilms to stick to your boat and make it their permanent home. Over time, you can have so many of them on your hull that the drag in the water from their bodies turns your speed boat into a bobbing cork. In fact, the growth of biofilms on commercial ships slows them down enough each year to cost the shipping and fishing industries one billion dollars annually. Thus, if you ever wonder why you paid extra for that authentic Hawaiian pineapple, just remember the unwelcome stowaways who came along for the ride—all courtesy of a biofilm.

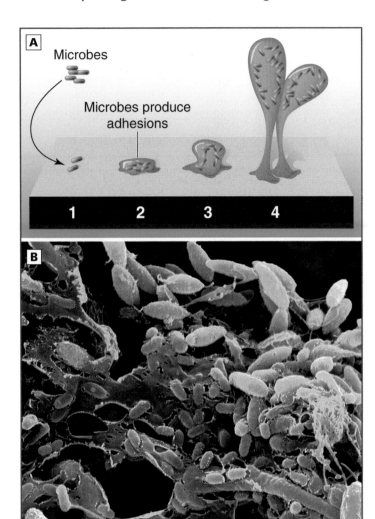

Figure 2.2 (A) Steps 1 through 4 of this illustration represent the typical stages in biofilm formation. In step 1, the microbe attaches to a surface using its external proteins. In step 2, the microbes use adhesions to glue themselves to the surface, causing metabolic changes (step 3) that allow the microbe to use the surface's resources to reproduce and grow (step 4). (B) Shown here is a typical example of a biofilm forming on a stainless steel surface, a material commonly used for surgical and other medical instruments.

biofilms unique, therefore, is not so much the general process or where they can form. Instead what distinguishes them from other kinds of biofilms is which specific proteins activate them and what metabolic changes this activation initiates. To see what these are, let's turn to look at how *C. albicans* does it.

HOW A FUNGUS INFECTS

As we have seen, the key to a biofilm is whether molecules on the outside of an organism match up with the molecules on the surface where it is trying to attach. Where the shape of one does not fit into the shape of the other, nothing happens. So to understand how *C. albicans* causes an infection, we need to know what specific "shape" on the surface of our cells activates it.

In the case of humans, the "shape" that sets things off is a group of proteins located on the outside of our cell membranes, called β_2 integrins. These proteins link the environment outside a given cell and its internal **cytoplasm**. They are one of the main ways cells communicate and link up with each other to form tissues. The part of this protein that extends outside the cell has a location on it where connecting molecules like **fibronectin** and **collagen** can attach. When one connecting molecule attaches to the β_2 integrins of two neighboring cells, it links them together. This connection then enables the two cells to communicate with one another and make each other perform different chemical reactions. In other words, β_2 integrins allow cells to talk and tell each other to change what they are doing from one task to the next. When this process is repeated between large numbers of cells, it creates a communication network of proteins. That enables cells with similar functions to fuse into a larger tissue. They then can work together to achieve a common task (e.g., making a muscle contract).

The role of β_2 integrins in our bodies, however, makes them the perfect "shape" to induce *C. albicans* to create a biofilm. *C. albicans* has evolved a protein on the outside of its cell wall that mimics the shape of the β_2 integrins. It is called "Int1p" (for "<u>Int</u>egrin found <u>1</u>st protein"). Yeasts that cannot produce Int1p are unable to attach to the surface of human tissues and are no longer **virulent.** But when Int1p is present, cells of *C. albicans* can bind to the human β_2 integrins (Figure 2.3). When they do, they cause the human cells to begin producing more of the connecting molecules to link up with other cells (since the host cells now "think" the Int1p proteins are new β_2 integrins that need connecting). All these extra connecting molecules, though, only serve as adhesins to glue the yeast cells to the human tissue surface.

Once this adherence occurs, the metabolic transformation of a biofilm is triggered. The invading fungal cells undergo a **morphogenesis** in which the yeast form of *C. albicans* transforms into a hyphae or filamentous form. These filaments dive down into the surrounding human tissue (Figure 2.4). There, they begin to release chemicals like phospholipase (a compound that destroys cell membranes) and aspartyl proteinase (a compound that chops up proteins). These degrading enzymes kill the human cells, allowing the fungus to absorb the resulting nutrients as food for its own growth. Thus, as the *C. albicans* biofilm forms, it uses the very surface it has attached to as the source for the food and raw materials it needs to spread and grow.

MEDICAL CHALLENGES

We can now see from this more detailed description of how *C. albicans* makes a biofilm what the general method of infection is for all fungi. First, each one of the infectious fungi has evolved proteins on the outside of their cell walls that match the shape of some important protein on the surface of human cell membranes. What is more, each kind infects a specific area of the body because only the tissues located there produce the specific trigger protein the fungus needs. Thus,

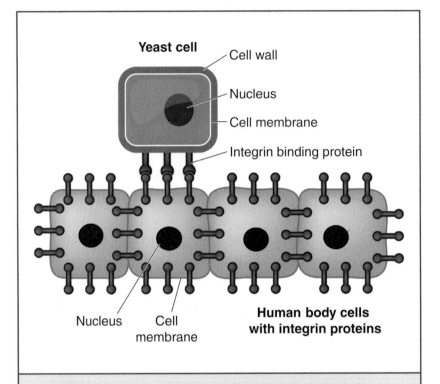

Figure 2.3 When a cell of *C. albicans* comes into contact with human tissue, proteins protrude from the outside surface, which enables it to bind to the cells of the tissue. These proteins have shapes that correspond to the shape of the beta-integrin proteins sticking out from the human cells. When the protein "puzzle pieces" match, the yeast can bind to the tissue.

athlete's foot, for example, does not appear in the lungs because the cells of the lungs do not produce the surface proteins of skin cells.

A second common feature with all infectious fungi is that they all cause the cells at the site of the invasion to act differently after the match up of the proteins. The invading fungi force the body's cells to produce proteins which aid in the binding process, turning the body into a co-conspirator in the manufacture of the biofilm.

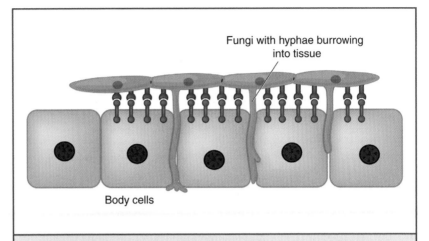

Figure 2.4 Following adhesion formation, the yeast cell transforms into a mold that begins to grow and extend its hyphae across the surface of the tissue. As the fungus expands, it produces hyphae that penetrate down between the cells of the tissue and begin to release the degrading enzymes that will kill the cells for food.

Finally, each of the infectious fungi undergoes a morphogenesis into a form that allows them to release degrading enzymes. As they stick to the tissue, they kill its cells and use these molecules and other chemicals for their own growth and reproduction. Put simply, the assaulting biofilm uses our bodies for food.

What all of this means for those suffering from a fungal infection is that they can be very difficult to treat. Cells in any biofilm are more resistant to **biocides, antiseptics,** and antibiotics because the arrangement of the cells creates layers where these drugs cannot penetrate. Only the microbes on the top surface of the biofilm get killed. But they are quickly replaced by those still permanently attached living below them. Therefore, anyone suffering an infection must reapply the treatment over and over again, often for many weeks, in order to wipe out all the layers of fungi. In extreme cases, they must even take medicine internally to try to disrupt the adhesion process itself on the surface of the tissue.

Long term exposure to antifungal drugs, though, is itself problematic. As noted in Chapter 1, most of the chemicals that kill fungi also harm us because we are both eukaryotes. So the fact that fungi infect by forming a biofilm forces patients to expose themselves to massive amounts of potentially toxic chemicals. It is why getting rid of an infectious fungus is so difficult (and after a certain point, nearly impossible). It is also why nosocomial infections so often result in death: anyone

A DIFFERENT KIND OF SCOURGE

Getting a fungal infection isn't the only way that yeast can hurt you. Among young children who live in poverty, *C. albicans* and its relatives are regularly behind one of the most familiar and frequent conditions in the world: diarrhea. A lack of food and the usual intestinal parasites change conditions in the gut, and the normal yeast that live there get out of control. The body's only line of defense is to try and flush them out. The result is a really bad case of diarrhea, and each year, millions of children around the world actually die from it. In fact, the dehydration associated with diarrhea caused by yeast is one of the leading killers of children in developing countries.

Adults and healthy children usually don't get diarrhea this way. Diarrhea is usually the result of microbes that have been ingested due to eating food that hasn't been properly cooked. The exception is when antibiotics are used. These drugs can kill both the natural and infectious bacteria in the intestines. The changes in your gut can then lead to just the sort of situation mentioned earlier. Your yeast get out of control. Your body tries to flush them out. And you spend a lot of time in the bathroom wondering what you've done to deserve all this.

in the hospital is already sick and weak; exposing them to potentially lethal drugs simply makes things worse.

Yet despite all these challenges, modern medicine is finding ways to combat infectious fungi, and the organism leading the way in this research is once again our "friend," *C. albicans*. Yeast infections are among the most common fungal diseases people encounter. In Chapter 3, we will look at how their symptoms and treatment provide a first glimpse into the world of infectious fungi.

3

Why Does It Itch?
Yeast Infections

In the late 1970s, doctors in New York City and San Francisco began to see a growing number of patients with a strange and unusual symptom. Otherwise healthy young men were coming to them with white fuzzy patches covering the insides of their mouths. Occasionally, they would complain that it was also painful to swallow. Puzzled, the doctors knew what to diagnose but not how to explain why these men had developed this condition. All of the patients had cases of a yeast infection known as oropharyngeal candidiasis, more commonly called "thrush." This disease is normally seen only in newborn infants or other people with weak immune systems. These men were all in their twenties, quite fit and active, and their bodies should have had no problem keeping the usual yeast populations in their mouths at bay. So what was going on?

What was happening, of course, was the beginning of the worst epidemic to strike humanity since the Black Plague swept across Europe in the Middle Ages. The young men were all victims of AIDS, and in the years that have followed, thrush has often been the first stage to an invasive, fatal case of infectious fungi. It—along with all the other fungal infections—has become the blight that has inflicted and eventually killed so many of them. Even now, yeast infections are the direct, final cause of death in the vast majority of AIDS cases in the United States[1] (see sidebar on page 31).

THE DISEASES

There are three basic diseases that humans can contract from infection with *Candida*. The first two—oropharyngeal candidiasis (**OPC**) and vulvovaginal candidiasis—are the more common of the three. Of these two, vaginal yeast infections are by far the most common, accounting for more than 90% of all cases of candidiasis. The third condition, known as candidemia,

AIDS AND YEAST

Sadly, AIDS and *Candida* have been constant companions from the very start. HIV, the virus that causes AIDS, kills off special white blood cells called helper T-cells. These T-cells control most of the immune system. As HIV kills T-cells, the body starts to lose its ability to fight back against invaders. Over time, a person infected with AIDS begins to suffer wave after wave of illnesses, until eventually the patient's body can't fight back anymore and he or she dies.

But with *Candida*, the body doesn't have to wait to bump into something that can infect it because the yeasts are already there. When someone acquires the AIDS virus, *Candida* are often the first thing to invade successfully, usually causing a fungal infection of the mouth called thrush. In fact, more than 70% of AIDS patients suffer from thrush at some point during the course of their illness. Worse, the yeast can enter the bloodstream where they attack the body's internal organs like the kidney. When this happens, a person can fall seriously ill and die.

While *Candida* are definitely one of the scourges AIDS sufferers have to deal with, these yeasts are not alone. In fact, HIV can harm the immune system so badly that even species of yeasts that *never* infect the body can cause illness. Even something as ordinary as baker's yeast for bread can cause an AIDS patient to get sick.

Furthermore, when medical treatment does control the *Candida,* other harmful fungi still wait in the wings for their own chance to invade, such as *Aspergillis, Histoplasma, and Cryptococcus.*

involves an invasive or systemic *Candida* yeast infection and is quite rare. We will discuss the first two in this chapter and save the third for later in Chapter 6 when we examine the other **opportunistic infections**.

The three diseases are all the product of a relatively small number of species of yeasts from the genus *Candida*. *C. albicans* is the most prevalent of them, causing nearly 70% of all infections. Hence, for simplicity's sake, we will assume throughout this book that members of this species are the causative agent. But other yeasts like *C. parapsilosis* and *C. krusei* have also been known to live in the digestive tract and the vagina and to flare up in quantity from time to time. It is these flare ups, of course, that actually cause the conditions, and they are all the result of ecological changes in the places where the yeasts normally live. *Candida* naturally inhabit the mucous linings of the mouth and vagina. They live there in small numbers, kept in check by other natural microbes living there as well as the body's own immune system. When something alters the chemistry or the physical conditions in these places, the yeasts there can breed excessively. Thus, for example, when fewer or weakened white blood cells roam the surface of the tongue and insides of your cheeks, this environmental change can result in thrush. Or when the acidity of the vagina goes down, the yeast there can produce a vaginal infection. In all cases (including candidemia), if you make life easier for the yeasts, they make life less easy for you.

Let's now take a closer look at thrush and vaginal yeast infections.

THRUSH

Historically, thrush has been found most commonly in newborns and the immunocompromised. The reason for this is that both groups of individuals have immune systems that do not function at peak capacity. In the case of newborns, their immune response has not yet fully developed. Hence, the white

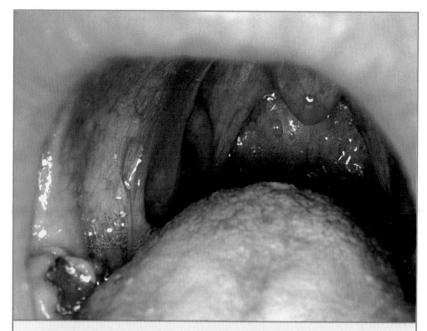

Figure 3.1 A typical case of thrush on the tongue with its characteristic white patches can be seen in this photograph.

blood cells, **antibodies**, and other immune enzymes do not always automatically recognize the *C. albicans* wandering around in their mouths. As a result, the *C. albicans* can reproduce faster than the immune system kills them off. In those babies where this happens, the excess population of yeast makes the child "catch" thrush.

The situation is slightly different in the immunocompromised. Here, a person's immune system has lost some of its ability to fight off invading microbes and viruses. Patients suffering from AIDS, for example, steadily lose their ability to direct an immune response as the HIV virus kills off the cells responsible for this process. Others, such as transplant patients, must actively suppress the immune response in order to help prevent the rejection of their new organs. In both cases, the immune system cannot kill *C. albicans* as effectively. Again, the population of yeasts can grow out of control, and when it does, the immunocompromised person will get thrush.

The symptoms of thrush are pretty basic. White, painless patches or spots start to form in the mouth, and they are commonly found on the back of the throat and tongue (Figure 3.1). When the patches form on the lining of the esophagus, they make swallowing painful. They are also a sign that the condition may be getting worse. Diagnosis consists of swabbing the patches and examining them with a microscope. When confirmed, the condition is usually treated with an oral **fungicide** like fluconazole, clotrimazole, or nystatin. Early treatment is important because thrush can easily lead in the immunocompromised to the more deadly and difficult to cure **systemic infection**, candidemia.

VAGINAL YEAST INFECTIONS

Other than ringworm (see Chapter 4), vaginal candidiasis—or as it is usually known, simply "yeast infection"—is the single most common infectious fungal condition there is. Like thrush, it arises because the *C. albicans* populations get out of hand—in this case in the vagina. But unlike thrush, what causes this explosion in reproduction has nothing to do with the immune system. Under normal circumstances, a woman's vagina excretes mucous that is quite acidic. This acidic fluid protects the entrance to the uterus by killing off microbes that try to enter from the outside. It also kills of some of the yeast cells as well and so keeps the population of *C. albicans* under control. In addition, there are bacteria which live in the mucous that kill and eat the yeast for food. This helps keep *C. albicans* numbers down even further. But when the vagina's mucous becomes less acidic, not as many yeast get killed. That allows for them to reproduce faster and more often, creating the potential for a population explosion that will lead to a yeast infection.

So what can change the vagina's environment? The most common answer is sexual activity. The semen men produce is alkaline in order to neutralize the acidity of the vagina's mucous (otherwise the acid would kill sperm as well as yeast). Furthermore, the skin of the penis introduces foreign bacteria that disrupt the general ecology of all the microbes living inside the vagina. Together, these factors can reduce the acidity enough to set off the overproduction of yeast. The more sexual activity a woman has, the more likely this change will happen and the more likely it is that she will get a yeast infection.

Other things that can change the acidity include the birth control pill, pregnancy, diabetes, and even antibiotics. Using too many broad spectrum antibiotics (those designed to kill a wide variety of bacteria) or using them too often can kill off the bacteria in the vagina's mucous. Hence, the bacteria which normally kill and eat the yeast are no longer there to do their job, allowing *C. albicans* to breed more. Too much stress has also been shown to cause yeast infections, and women involved in a military deployment are particularly prone to getting them.

Regardless of how it happens, however, yeast infections are a reality most women will have to cope with at some point in their lives. About 75% of all women will get at least one yeast infection in her life, and half of them will get more than one. Some women have even been known to have as many as four or more attacks per year. For obvious reasons, it is rare for celibate women and girls who haven't undergone puberty to get one. But for most adult women, yeast infections are one of the most common reasons why they visit their primary care physician or gynecologist.

What prompts a woman to go to the doctor is usually one of several possible symptoms. Usually there is an itching or burning sensation in her vagina. In addition, her discharge from her vagina may appear like thick cottage cheese in its texture and color. Sexual intercourse often becomes painful, and the vulva or flaps of tissue surrounding the opening to the vagina (Figure 3.2) can become swollen. In extreme cases, an actual rash breaks out in the vagina and is extremely itchy.

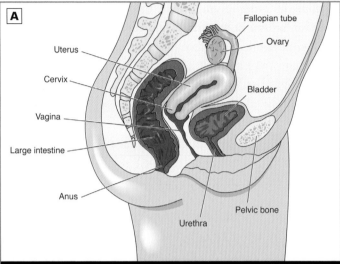

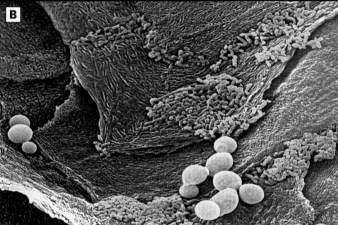

Figure 3.2 (A) Vaginal yeast infections can occur anywhere within the vulva region, extending from the opening of the urethra all the way to the anus. They usually occur just inside the vagina's opening or the tissue immediately surrounding it. (B) This microscopic picture, taken with a scanning electron microscope and magnified 7,000 times, shows usual yeast activity in the vagina. Yeast are a normal part of the vagina, and together with bacteria (in blue), they comprise its natural environment. Only when something disrupts this environment can the yeast grow out of control and cause an infection.

To treat a yeast infection, it is important first to get a correct diagnosis. Bacterial infections of a women's urinary tract can cause similar symptoms, and since the discharge does not always appear, it is possible for a woman to assume wrongly that she has a yeast infection. Treatment for the two conditions, though, uses completely different medicines. Therefore, any woman suffering from itching or burning sensations in her genital region needs to see a doctor to determine the actual cause.

Diagnosis and treatment for a yeast infection are pretty straightforward. The doctor swabs the vaginal opening to collect a sample of the fluid or discharge. Then he or she either smears the swab on a microscope slide for examination or places it in growth medium to culture for any possible *C. albicans* that might be present. Once the yeast are observed, the patient usually will be given one of the commercially available over-the-counter **azole** drugs (see Chapter 8). The most common brand names are Gyne-Lotrimin and Monistat 7, and they usually come in the form of a cream or suppository. The patient applies these drugs directly to the infected area over a period of usually 7 to 10 days until the symptoms go away. In severe cases, she may also need to take oral medication as well.

Because yeast infections can occur so regularly in women, one of the most important steps a woman can take is prevention. She should avoid wearing tight-fitting clothing or clothes made from synthetic fibers. These items can trap excess moisture around the genitals which neutralizes the acidity of the vagina. For this same reason, it is important to remove a wet bathing suit promptly as well. Women should avoid deodorant sanitary pads or tampons, and when bathing, they should avoid bath oils and be sure to dry themselves thoroughly afterwards. Douches and feminine hygiene sprays should not be used because like sexual activity, they can upset the vagina's ecological balance. Finally, over-the-counter treatments should only be used *after* a correct diagnosis.

This last method for prevention is particularly important because each time a woman uses an antifungal drug, she creates resistance in those yeasts which do survive. Drug resistance is also why following preventive steps is so important to a woman's long-term health. The more often she can avoid contracting a yeast infection, the less often she will need to treat one and the more likely it is that whatever drug she uses will work.

We will examine the issues of drug resistance more in Chapter 8, but for now, we will turn first to discuss the other four major groups of infectious fungal diseases: the **cutaneous** or superficial **mycoses** (Chapter 4), the **subcutaneous** mycoses (Chapter 5), the opportunistic systemic mycoses (Chapter 6), and the non-opportunistic systemic mycoses (Chapter 7).

4

Ringworm and Other Superficial Mycoses

You are so excited! You are picking up your new kitten from the animal shelter today. You just can not wait to hold her and play with her. You have already made a place for her in your room (though secretly you hope she'll sleep with you). You have all the kitty toys purchased and ready for play, and you have assured your mother repeatedly that you *will* take care of the litter box. When you arrive at the shelter, the kitten immediately snuggles up against you, purring, and you just know the two of you will become inseparable companions forever. Later, as she nestles against your neck to settle down for the night, you give a small, contented smile and drift off to sleep yourself. You wonder how your feelings for her could ever change.

A few weeks later, though, you find yourself starting to scratch your neck where she sleeps. In a couple of days you start to notice your skin there is becoming kind of flaky. The itching gets worse, and the flakes start to form small, ring shaped patterns. You worry that your kitten might catch whatever you have. So you force her to sleep outside your room, even though her painful cries for attention tug at your heart. You also start to grow concerned because your neck is starting to look kind of ugly and you've got a major college interview coming up. You try washing and swabbing the area with alcohol. But finally, when the sores become moist and crusty, you break down and go to your doctor. There, you learn the worst news of all: your beloved pet has given you **ringworm**. The thought of a worm crawling around on you makes you shudder, but you doctor explains that what you have really caught is a fungus, called "ringworm" because of the ring like shape of the rash. You're not too thrilled at the thought of a fungus on your skin either. But then you wonder: How could either your pet or you get a fungus on your skin in the first place?

CUTANEOUS MYCOSES

The most common of all fungal infections are those involving the skin. A group of molds formally known as the **dermatophytes** cause them, and the species involved all come from either the genus *Trichophyton*, *Microsporum*, or *Epidermophyton*. Interestingly, any of these species can cause a different **tinea** (the common term for the conditions) depending on where on the skin the fungus invades. As a result, doctors use a tinea's specific location to make a diagnosis rather than according to what species actually causes it (e.g., tinea corporis is body ringworm while tinea capitis is scalp ringworm).

To contract one of these conditions, a person must come into direct contact with people or pets who have already been infected. Or they must come into contact with objects like towels and hairbrushes that an infected individual has used. Those caught from pets or other animals tend to produce more inflammatory **lesions** than the ones caught from other people. But the severity of any tinea varies dramatically from one individual to the next no matter what its source.

The reason why, ironically, is that the general **pathology** for the numerous cutaneous mycoses is pretty much the same. Damp, humid conditions (such as a sweaty foot in a shoe) create an environment where the fungi can become a biofilm. This biofilm grows on the outermost layer of the **epidermis** of the skin called the "stratum corneum" (or sometimes inside the hair follicles). As it does so, the fungal hyphae burrow down into the skin, causing inflammation, scaling, and occasionally itching. What then determines the severity of this inflammation, scaling, etc. is how well an individual sufferer's immune system responds to the infection. Most of us will usually only experience a few patches of dry, flaky skin and at most, minor discomfort. In fact, children younger than five years old seldom catch a tinea because their immune system is so active during this period.

But some people seem genetically predisposed to have worse symptoms because their immune systems do not recognize the fungus as a foreign body. These individuals experience dramatic swelling and often painful itching, and the disease will regularly spread over large areas of their bodies. In the worst cases, a person's immune response may be so weak that the body actually learns to live with the species of fungus and no longer actively fights it. The infection then becomes chronic and a permanent part of that individual's life (certain diabetics are particularly prone to such tineas).

One thing that can happen with all tineas, though, is secondary infection. When one of these infections occurs in areas where the stratum corneum is thicker (particularly in the spaces between the fingers and toes), bacteria can join the fungus invasion. What happens is that the fungal biofilm in these areas can burrow down deeper. The extra dead, decaying cells then provide the resources bacteria need to begin reproducing in greater numbers, too. Thus, instead of just a fungal biofilm, the patient now has a multi-microbial biofilm that can require a wide variety of drugs to fight it, making the condition much harder to combat. Infections like athlete's foot (tinea pedis) are often quite difficult to cure for just this reason.

TYPES AND TREATMENTS
Scientists classify the fungal infections of the skin according to how deeply they penetrate the skin. The true cutaneous mycoses are those which invade the full stratum corneum of

the epidermis. These include true ringworm (called that because many of the tineas are often accidentally misdiagnosed as this condition) and athlete's foot. The superficial mycoses are the other category, and while the fungi that cause them do attack the hair and skin, they do not penetrate more than a few cells deep. As a consequence, they produce significantly milder symptoms (see Table 4.1 for a summary of the various fungal skin diseases).

Table 4.1 The Cutaneous and Superficial Mycoses

CONDITION	COMMON NAME	LOCATION ON BODY	MAJOR SYMPTOM
Tinea corporis	ringworm	any skin surface except scalp, feet, and male facial areas	flaky sores with well-defined ring shapes
Tinea capitis	cradle cap	scalp	scaly, swollen blisters or rash of "black dots"
Tinea cruris	jock itch	genitals, buttocks, and inner thighs	raised red sores with well-defined edges
Tinea unguium	nail fungus	nail bed of toes and rarely fingers	thickened, discolored nail
Tinea pedis	athlete's foot	toes and soles of feet	red flaky rash
Piedraia hortai	Black piedra	scalp hair	hair loss from broken hair shafts
Trichosporon beigelii	White piedra	pubic, beard, eyebrow, and eyelash hair	hair loss from broken hair shafts
Tinea nigra	———	any skin surface	red flaky patches
Tinea versicolor	———	any skin surface	red flaky patches

The symptoms for the different conditions (except tinea unguium and the piedras) all involve variations on a central theme. In each, the skin becomes inflamed and itchy, with rash like welts or sores. The texture of these sores is then usually flaky or scaly, and their specific shape can determine the diagnosis. Thus, tinea corporis or true ringworm has the classic ring shape for which it is known (Figure 4.1) while tinea cruris or "jock itch" produces raised red sores with well-defined edges. The other infections produce more uneven patterns on the skin. Hence, their diagnosis depends entirely on the location and texture of the infection.

Some of the tineas have changing symptoms as the disease progresses. For instance, the fungal infection of the scalp known as tinea capitis or cradle cap can begin as a rash of black-looking dots that evolve into scaly swollen blisters. Left untreated, these blisters can become filled with pus, resulting in crusting, flaking, and round bald patches on the scalp (Figure 4.2). Permanent scarring and hair loss is possible. Tinea capitis is most common among African American children, making it unusual in that it tends to affect one ethnic group more than others.

Tinea unguium and the piedras (superficial mycoses caused by common white and black molds) are different from the rest of the fungal infections of the skin. Many of the other kinds—in addition to similar symptoms—also have the potential if left untreated to penetrate into the blood stream. There, they can eventually lead to more widespread, systemic infections, particularly in the immunocompromised. But tinea unguium or nail fungus (along with the piedras and the two superficial tineas) can never threaten the actual life of their hosts. They are strictly cosmetically annoying. In the case of nail fungus, for example, one of the victim's toenails (usually on the big toe) starts to thicken and turn a tarnished white or yellow color. The fungus spreads down the nail from its tip, until the nail slowly deteriorates, breaks apart, and falls off. It

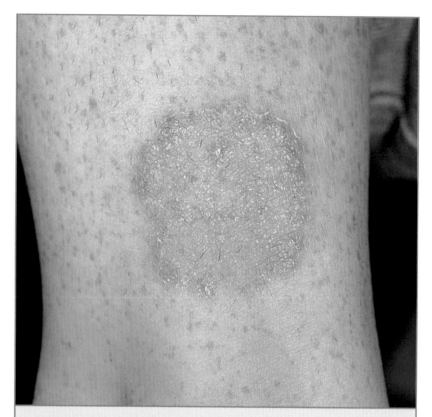

Figure 4.1 A typical example of tinea corporis is shown here. Note the circular nature of the infection; hence the common name for the condition, ringworm.

can then spread to other toes on the foot, and while the process is painless and harmless to the rest of the body, the results can be quite repulsive (Figure 4.3). Black and white piedra, tinea nigra, and tinea versicolor produce similar blemishing of the hair and skin (Figure 4.4). Thus, even though none of these conditions pose any real threat to someone's health, most people seek treatment for them simply because they can make you look unattractive.

Yet treating these or any other of the fungi that infect the skin can prove quite tricky. While some just appear and

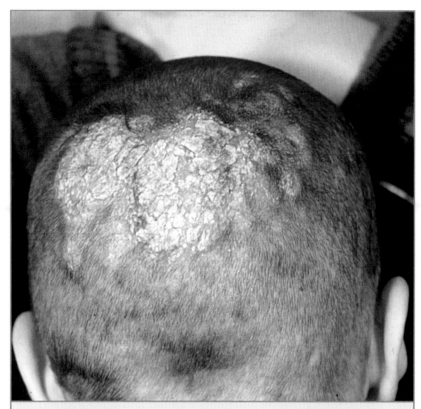

Figure 4.2 Tinea capitis or cradle cap appears most often in children. An abnormally itchy scalp is the most common symptom. Balding patches, as seen here, usually confirm the diagnosis.

disappear within weeks without any therapy, others can take as much as a year to cure. Most require some kind of topical, over-the-counter antifungal medication, but a few need oral drugs as well. Patients usually have to use any of the different medications for at least two weeks *after* the lesions disappear in order to make certain that all the fungal cells have died, and the basic procedure in all cases is pretty much the same. With ringworm, the patient must wear loose clothing and apply antifungal ointment to the skin. For jock itch, a person should wear cotton underwear (changing it several times a

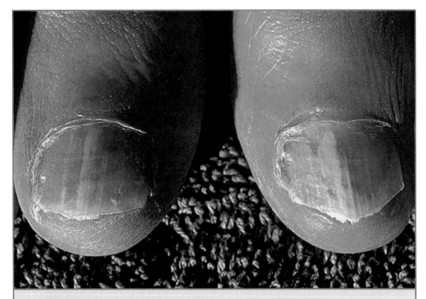

Figure 4.3 A case of nail fungus, though cosmetically unappealing, is painless and harmless. It is also quite challenging to cure and can take several months of using topical over-the-counter drugs to treat the condition.

day) and use both an antifungal powder and ointment on the infected region. Cradle cap sufferers have to rely on prescription shampoos (or in severe cases take oral medication), and someone infected with nail fungus can apply topical over-the-counter drugs (effective 40%–50% of the time) or take oral azoles (see Chapter 8). In all cases, any clothing, nail clippers, towels, hairbrushes or other objects which come in contact with the infected site must be boiled to disinfect and sterilize them.

Yet even with these steps, recurrence of infections that do not just disappear on their own is quite common. One in five of the skin conditions develops into a chronic infection, and nail fungi come back 75% of the time. As a matter of fact, nail fungi are the limpets of the fungus world, tenaciously hanging on no matter what medications are thrown at them. Even

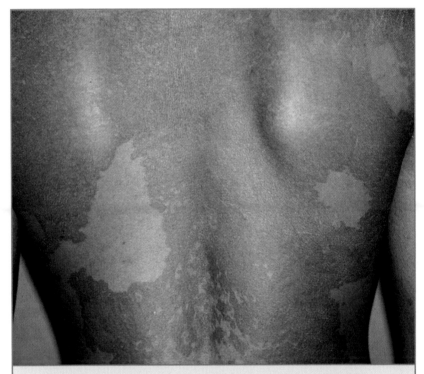

Figure 4.4 The fungus *Malassezia furfur* can cause blotches on the skin known as tinea versicolor. While this infection looks bad, like all of the superficial mycoses, it seldom threatens the patient's health and usually clears up on its own.

when the oral azoles are used (which are so potentially harmful to the liver and kidneys they require a blood test before a doctor will prescribe them), it can take 3 to 12 months to "cure" an existing infection.

But why? Modern science now believes that people with nail fungi or any other recurring fungal skin condition probably have a defect in their immune systems. The hypothesis is that the white bloods cells in these individuals must be missing some type of genetic information and that this missing information prevents their immune cells from always recognizing the invading fungus as foreign. As a consequence, the immune system does not consistently attack these fungi, and so once a person has contracted a cutaneous fungus, they must pretty much cope with it for life—not a pleasant prospect when you have to keep using ever more expensive and hazardous medicines (see Chapter 8).

As with any disease or infection, therefore, prevention is the key. Fortunately with cutaneous and superficial mycoses, it is a pretty easy thing to do (see sidebar). Basic hygiene suppresses any initial formation of fungal biofilm. Hence, if a

PREVENTING INFECTION

The best way to cope with any of the tineas is prevention, and the key to that is good personal hygiene. Damp, humid, and dirty conditions are just what these fungi are looking for, and so avoiding these conditions goes a long way toward keeping you healthy and itch free. Whenever you shower or bathe, make sure to dry extra carefully between your fingers and toes and your genital area. Don't share towels, and don't go around barefoot in locker rooms or public showers—wear some waterproof sandals instead.

Actually, sandals are a good staple because they keep your feet nice and dry. But when you do have to wear shoes, you should change socks regularly, consider some kind of absorbent powder, and keep your nails clipped short to keep them from trapping any moisture under them. Wear loose clothing and use styling gels sparingly (which slow the evaporation of sweat from your head and trap its moisture there) to keep your skin and hair cool and dry. Tightly braided hair also traps moisture against your head, and immersing your bare hands in water for prolonged periods can also expose your skin to too much moisture. The bottom line is, by keeping the surface of your skin clean and dry, you keep your skin healthy and happy. Or to put it another way: a shower a day keeps the dermatologist at bay.

person does come in contact with an individual *Trichophyton* or *Microsporum*, the cells of the fungus can't get a beachhead. The immune system then readily takes care of killing them off. Only when dirt and other particulate matter trap moisture against the skin's surface does the necessary environmental change occur to enable construction of the biofilm and the resulting infection. So while cleanliness may or may not be next to godliness, in the case of skin fungi, it certainly determines healthiness.

5

Getting Under Your Skin— Subcutaneous Conditions

As we mentioned in Chapter 1, most fungi don't need or use humans in order to reproduce and live successfully in the environment. Consequently, the vast majority of them we "bump into" each day do exactly that: like strangers encountering each other in a subway, the fungi bump up against us by landing on our skin, perhaps "ride around" on us for a while, and then eventually leave as they get brushed or washed off. Neither organism is ever aware of the other. Like atmospheric pressure and a person's beating heart, these daily encounters remain nothing but biological "background noise."

However, sometimes when we "bump" into a fungus, we also "bump" into something else, like a thorn on a bush or the rough bark of a tree. Then the fungus can penetrate the skin and encounter a new and different environment, which can lead to what by now should be a familiar pattern: altering the environment alters the character of the fungus and the infection can begin.

The diseases we will be looking at in this chapter all share this common cause. They are always the result of an **inoculation** through a puncture or open wound. All of them usually remain localized to the immediate site of the injury. But when an infection does spread, it does so very slowly through the passageways of the body's **lymphatic system** which are in direct contact with the wound. The result is that even when these conditions do spread, they almost always remain confined to a single body part or limb.

Because injury is necessary to cause one of these infections, the fungi species involved vary dramatically, simply depending on what kind are present in the environment where and when the wound occurs. Hence, unlike the yeast and tinea conditions, the different subcutaneous infections do not come from a common genus or share any immediate genetic relationships. As a consequence, there are literally dozens of different kinds of subcutaneous fungal infections. This can make treatment quite tricky because doctors must determine which specific fungus is causing the illness in order to target it with the right medication. Since the symptoms are often similar, problems with identification makes this challenge even more acute.

Of course, the obvious thing to do is to prevent infection in the first place. Simply cleaning wounds thoroughly and promptly keeps potentially infectious fungi from doing any harm almost 100% of the time. In fact, poor hygiene is one of the reasons most people who become infected with a subcutaneous fungal condition are usually from either tropical or economically disadvantaged regions. The necessary cleanliness is simply more challenging in those places (see sidebar on page 52). In the U.S. and Northern Europe, on the other hand, the conditions we will discuss in this chapter do not occur as often because clean water and proper hygiene are readily available. When they do occur, it is almost always in individuals who are immunocompromised or who were at high risk because of their type of work.

Let us turn now to look at the four known subcutaneous fungal infections.

SPOROTRICHOSIS

Sporothrix schenckii is a mold commonly found living in the soil and on the surface of plants and plant material. Normally, it is a simple saprobe, decomposing dead or dying plant material. Common sources for it include rose bushes, sphagnum moss (the kind covering peat bogs), and bailed hay. But when it gains access to the inside of our bodies, our higher internal temperature causes the mold to convert to a yeast. This yeast then starts to generate a biofilm along the linings of the

WHEN DISASTER STRIKES

On December 26, 2004, one of the worst tsunamis in recorded history struck the beaches of the Indian Ocean. Plowing miles inland, the waves washed away entire towns, changing the shape of those shorelines forever. Millions of survivors found themselves homeless, jobless, and penniless. The devastation will take decades to repair.

Unfortunately, lack of drinking water, food, and shelter would be only the beginning for the sufferers of the tsunami. Into all that devastation, the waves released other foes as well—infectious fungi.

Natural disasters like the 2004 tsunami do far more than wipe out lives and homes. They also set the perfect stage for the kinds of fungal infections discussed in this chapter. Smashing waves cause scrapes and cuts. Torn debris punctures unprotected feet. Crushed plants and animals rot in the mud and sun, releasing mounting numbers of mold spores. All of these factors expose disaster victims to the culprits responsible for diseases like Madura foot and zygomycosis. Sterile water and soap needed to clean wounds and prevent infection have been destroyed as well.

To make matters worse, these disasters wipe out the infrastructure needed to deliver drugs and medical services. So long after the waves have retreated or the earth has stopped shaking or the typhoon has stopped blowing, the victims of these disasters have far more to cope with than just rebuilding their lives and their societies. They face personal battles against some of nature's nastiest foes.

lymph vessels at the site of the wound. The initial symptoms appear as insect bite-like welts on the surface of the skin. But over time, these welts develop into a chain of ulcerated lesions along the surface of the injured skin (Figure 5.1). Known as **sporotrichosis**, this condition will persist if left untreated for a very long time. Even with the consumption of oral potassium iodide (the standard treatment), it heals slowly and can spread from the site of the initial inoculation, growing along the lymph vessels draining that one region of the body (Figure 5.2). But it is extremely rare that the fungus moves beyond the lymph node region where the condition originates. However, in the immunocompromised, it can often spread to the lungs, spinal cord, and brain, causing a systemic infection.

Because nurseries and greenhouses commonly use the plants on which *S. schenckii* lives, outbreaks of sporotrichosis are most common among people who work in these facilities (though for some unknown reason, children acquire it more often from hay). Those at extra risk, such as florists, also work regularly with sphagnum moss. *S. schenckii* has a high affinity for this moss and in its native environment decays the sphagnum into peat. But the moss is highly water absorbent, making it ideal for lining wire baskets, making wreaths, storing seeds, or any other situation that needs something kept well watered. Those who work with it need to take extra care to follow the usual precautions that everyone who works regularly with plants should follow: to avoid contamination with *S. schenckii*, wear gloves, long sleeves, and sturdy jeans to prevent punctures, scrapes, and cuts and wash any injuries that still might occur thoroughly with soap and water.

CHROMOBLASTOMYCOSIS

The four most common fungi that cause this disease (*Cladophialophora carrionii, Fonsecaea compacta, Fonsecaea pedrosoi, Phialophora verrucosa*) occur in soils and on decaying plant material around the world. Yet the majority of cases

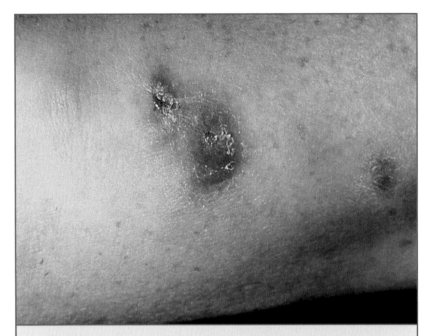

Figure 5.1 This typical example of sporotrichosis shows the classic ulcerations of the skin commonly associated with this condition.

of **chromoblastomycosis** occur among bare-footed populations who live in the tropics, and incidents are highest in people who live on the islands of the South Pacific.

Infection happens when the fungus enters through a cut or splinter, usually on the foot or leg, and the first symptoms of it are a small firm bump that is either red or gray in color. This bump will often go unnoticed for quite a while because the various species of fungi responsible for the condition grow and reproduce much more slowly than the other infectious fungi. The initial red or gray bump will only increase in size about 2 mm per year, and both sufferers and doctors have been known to confuse the small, sometimes itchy, bump for some other common skin condition, including an insect bite. Eventually, the fungal biofilm enlarges enough to form an itchy, warty nodule that can rise off the skin as much as 3 cm

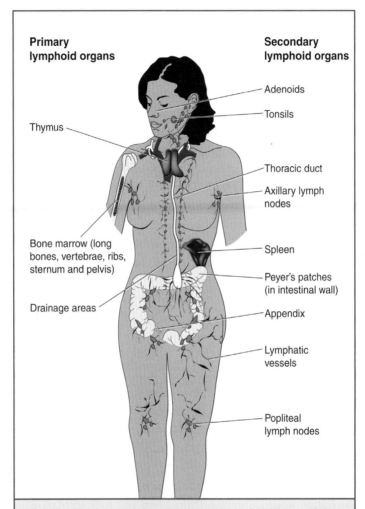

Primary lymphoid organs

Thymus

Bone marrow (long bones, vertebrae, ribs, sternum and pelvis)

Drainage areas

Secondary lymphoid organs

Adenoids

Tonsils

Thoracic duct

Axillary lymph nodes

Spleen

Peyer's patches (in intestinal wall)

Appendix

Lymphatic vessels

Popliteal lymph nodes

Figure 5.2 A common feature of all the subcutaneous fungal infections is their ability to use the body's lymphatic system to spread beyond the initial inoculation site. Consisting of a series of vessels that recapture liquid lost from the blood, the system drains this liquid into nodes where it is filtered and returned to the blood. Various fungi species use the lymph vessels like highways to travel and infect other areas of the skin connected to the vessel where the fungus first enters the body. They cannot, however, usually move beyond a node, and so there is a limit to how far the fungi can spread their infections.

(Figure 5.3), and if left untreated, the disease can grow after many years into a large, cauliflower shaped growth protruding from the skin.

ANCIENT ENEMIES

Plants and fungi have been doing battle for hundreds of millions of years. While some soil fungi help plants (see sidebar on page 14 in Chapter 1), many others simply see our green friends as just another food source. There are species that attack the roots. There are species that attack the stem. There are others that attack the leaves. Mildews, blights, and rusts burrow their hyphae into the flesh of the plant just like *S. schenckii* and its *Acremonium* cousins can dig into ours. They form biofilms; release their degrading enzymes, and munch away.

These fungi also almost always kill. Plants don't have as sophisticated an immune system as animals, so when a plant catches a fungal infection, it almost never survives. Sometimes, this can have devastating consequences not only for the individual plant but also for entire ecosystems. Dutch elm disease and chestnut blight have all but wiped out elms and American chestnut trees from the eastern half of the United States. Organisms that depended on these trees have had to adapt to their absence, and the forests in this part of the U.S. will never be the same again.

Fungi that infect plants have also had a profound impact on people. Because so much of our food comes from crops we grow, we can run into real trouble if a fungus attacks them. The famous potato famine in Ireland in 1846 came about because potato blight wiped out all the potatoes in the entire country in one week! This famine changed the very history of Europe and the U.S. as millions died and millions more emigrated. Fungi have even threatened entire ways of life when in the late 19th century, downy mildew almost wiped out the French wine industry.

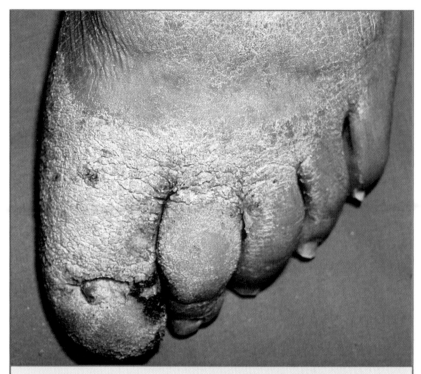

Figure 5.3 This case of chromoblastomycosis displays the wart-like symptoms typical of a developed infection. If this person leaves the condition untreated any longer, a cauliflower shaped tumor will eventually begin to grow off the surface of the skin.

While the fungal biofilm usually remains confined to the site of the inoculation, it can spread through the lymph ducts to the local nodes in the area. Excessive scratching can also spread the fungus, and in the immunocompromised, the fungus can travel through the blood to the brain where it eats holes in the nerve tissue, turning the brain into something that looks like Swiss cheese. In long standing cases of many years or more, chromoblastomycosis can also in rare instances trigger **squamous cell carcinoma**—a type of skin cancer—to develop at the site of the infection, adding to the challenges of treatment.

And treatment is quite challenging. Although science has documented cases of this disease resolving themselves spontaneously, chromoblastomycosis almost always requires direct medical intervention that is extremely difficult and prolonged. Sometimes, when a doctor diagnoses the disease at its earliest stages, he or she can prescribe one of the topical antifungals. But the drugs take 6–12 months to work and often fail to cure it anyway. Usually, along with medication, the patient requires surgery to cut the fungal growth out (using either a traditional scalpel or one of the newer methods of freezing and burning it away with liquid nitrogen). The surgeon must remove not only the fungus but a significant amount of the surrounding "healthy" tissue as well because it is the only way to guarantee that all of the fungus has actually been removed. Yet, the resulting large, open wound can take a long time to heal, especially in places where the disease is quite common. Poor or inadequate hygiene conditions in the tropics make the surgical wound an ideal breeding ground for bacteria, and secondary infections regularly add to the recovery time.

MADURA FOOT

The first reported case of **Madura foot** (more formally known as **mycetoma**) was in 1934 in Brazil. To this day, cases of it occur almost exclusively in tropical areas, and outbreaks are most often prevalent following natural disasters. Its source is a group of species of black and white molds from the genus *Acremonium* that produce a chronic, tumor-like swelling of the foot with numerous red and swollen lesions. Within these lesions is a network of large open sinuses or open pockets of space in the tissue where the fungus reproduces and enlarged cavities where the pus and decayed tissue from fighting the infection drain.

Oddly enough, Madura foot usually produces only a mild discomfort to the sufferer. But the danger in that is that it can cause the patient to delay treatment, which can prove critical.

This infection requires early and very specific intervention. Without the use of oral azoles targeted at whichever unique species of fungus has caused the infection (there are several), the disease can spread into the sinuses of the bones of the foot. There, the hyphae of the fungi begin to penetrate and eat away at the bone tissue itself. Over time, the actual structure and architecture of the foot can collapse, leaving what amounts to a rubble of bone chips inside the fleshy bag of the foot's skin.

Sadly, diagnosis of this condition usually does not take place until the tumor-like swelling becomes evident. At that stage, the fungus does not respond well to medicinal treatment. In addition, because Madura foot is mainly a tropical disease, most who contract it do not have access to adequate medical care or facilities anyway. As a result, amputation of the infected foot or lower limb is regularly the only option available.

ZYGOMYCOSIS

The condition **zygomycosis** is somewhat unusual because it is acute rather than chronic. Any number of soil molds and those found on decaying vegetation can cause it, and most are from the genera *Mucor, Absidia, or Cunninghamella.* Interestingly (and for reasons not yet understood), cases of it occur most in sufferers of type I diabetes (where the body can no longer produce insulin).

As with Madura foot, the cases tend to increase following a severe natural disaster. But the spread of the mold through the body is much more rapid. Entering through the nasal passages, it spreads rapidly to the eye and through the optic nerve channel to the brain. Or if it enters directly through the skin, it moves rapidly through the blood to colonize the kidney. In both cases, the organism destroys the infected tissues, feeding off them and reproducing prolifically. Within only a few days of inoculation, the patient either slips into a coma or undergoes total kidney failure.

Like all of the subcutaneous fungal infections, this also requires a very precise drug regimen. Without it, patients die within hours of onset of the coma or kidney failure. But unlike the other conditions, the acute nature of this disease makes it nearly impossible to diagnose in time—particularly in developing countries because of the poor medical situation in the first place. Hence, most who contract this disease die from it.

6

Kick 'em When They're Down— Opportunistic Fungi

In a hospital in London, a 45-year-old woman checks into the emergency room complaining of a chronic dry cough and a sore throat. The intern taking her medical history learns that she has had treatment for breast cancer. She had to have her left breast removed, and she received radiation therapy for a tumor which had spread to her lung. But when asked how she is feeling now, the woman says that she is fine except for this cough and sore throat. Further inquiry reveals that she has been disease free for four years, doesn't smoke, and has had no other respiratory problems of any kind until now.

Puzzled, the intern knows that with any other patient and such common symptoms, he would simply diagnose a probable bacterial infection. He would prescribe some antibiotics and send her home. But the cancer history makes him cautious. So he sends for her medical records from the **oncology** ward. When they arrive, he notices that an earlier chest x-ray shows a lesion on the left side where something has carved out a deep depression in the lung tissue. He begins to wonder if she might have contracted a case of tuberculosis or pneumonia.

Meanwhile, however, the patient's cough has grown more severe. She begins to have trouble breathing. Within a matter of hours, she is suffering severe respiratory distress. Her chest and abdomen shudder with spasms as she gasps for breath. The intern orders intravenous steroids to stop the swelling. But her vocal chords eventually become so inflamed they entirely shut off her air passageway. The medical team—which now includes the senior resident—has to perform an emergency **tracheotomy,** and they immediately admit the woman into Intensive Care.

While the woman lies unconscious, wheezing through the tube protruding from her throat, the senior resident orders broad-spectrum antibiotics. A nurse hooks up an IV to deliver the drugs directly into her blood stream, and for 26 days, the antibiotics drip steadily into her body. Yet for 26 days, her condition grows steadily worse. Finally, the doctors perform a bronchoscopy, sending the camera down into her lungs to take a look. What they discover is astonishing. All along the lining of her trachea near where it branches into the bronchi, dead strands of lung tissue hang and flutter like streamers from a wall. What looks like a small forest of mushrooms partially block the right bronchus. A CT scan confirms similar features where the old lesion in the left lung was, and suddenly, the medical team knows that it has been fighting the wrong pathogen. Desperately, they change the patient's medication, but it is too late. Eight days later, the woman dies.

GENERAL OVERVIEW

What happened to this woman? The short answer is that she died of a fungal infection. But the long answer is more elaborate and, scientifically, more interesting. She was the victim of a unique group of fungal diseases caused by what are known as the **opportunistic fungi.** These are fungi that are able to take advantage of people with damaged or preoccupied immune responses (such as having to fight cancer). They use this "opportunity" to invade the interior of the body and use it as a nutritional resource. The result is a systemic infection in which the fungi attack entire groups of organs and tissues via the blood stream, making the entire body ill. Almost all of these fungi enter through the lungs when people inhale their spores, and the numerous species involved exist everywhere in every environment throughout the world.

Because these fungi take advantage of weakened immune responses, the vast majority of cases of opportunistic fungal infections are nosocomial. Patients in hospitals are by definition people who's immune systems are already preoccupied fighting something else. So they are already prone to catch these diseases. But with medical advances in the past twenty years, patients with very weakened immune systems—including those who are fully immunocompromised by AIDS or organ trans-plantation—are living longer. Therefore, more and more patients in hospitals are contracting opportunistic fungal infections. They are spending longer and longer periods of time in the hospital fighting something other than what brought them in in the first place. As a matter of fact, the leading cause for increased hospitalization and mortality rates in the immunocompromised is *solely* the opportunistic fungi.

Obviously, since pathogens of any kind can take advantage of an over stressed immune system, any of the fungi men-tioned in this book *could* cause a systemic infection of the opportunistic kind. Even traditionally harmless organisms like *Saccharaomyces cerevisiae* (ordinary baker's yeast) have caused such infections when the immune system is compromised enough. For our purposes, though, we will concentrate on the four most common of the opportunistic systemic infections in this chapter and examine only **aspergillosis, cryptococcosis, pneumocystosis,** and **candidemia** in detail.

ASPERGILLOSIS

The leading killers in the category of opportunistic fungi are definitely *Aspergillis fumigatus* and *A. flavus*. These common saprobes regularly find their way from the soil into the air and into people's lung. Up to two out of every 100,000 people annually catch a case of aspergillosis, and this number is grow-ing as our society ages. The disease usually enters through the lung, but it has been known to colonize burn wounds and even enter through the ear canal. Most who suffer its more extreme symptoms are already coping with some kind of other lung condition like tuberculosis or cancer. Among the latter, only candidemia (discussed later) occurs more often as a secondary infection, and for people with AIDS, the disease is a regular killer.

The general pathology of both species is the same. Once inhaled, the spores transform into molds which begin to grow

FUNGAL KERATITIS

Weak immune systems are not the only vulnerable areas that risk attack from *Aspergillis* molds. In the tropical and subtropical parts of the world, these fungi are notorious for attacking perfectly healthy people, but not in the lungs. No, in this part of the world, *Aspergillis* likes the surface of the eye, and for those with injured corneas, this mold takes no prisoners. *Aspergillis* is difficult to treat and causes one of the most destructive eye infections known to science. A leading cause of blindness among farmers from this region, 50% of those infected have vision so damaged that they can barely count their own fingers when held right in front of their faces.

An infection caused by *Aspergillis* is also quite uncomfortable. Direct light hurts, eyes constantly tear, and the itching and swelling can be unbearable. To make matters worse, drugs that can help with the swelling and pain actually help the fungus grow! Even crueler, the drugs that do work are almost as corrosive as the mold.

The only way to stop the infection is through surgery. An ophthalmologist cuts deep trenches in the cornea around the existing infection to prevent the fungus from spreading. This way, only the infected parts of the cornea die and scar over the incision. As a result of the surgery, sight is not as acute, but the fungal damage is contained.

biofilms along the lining of the lung's airways (Figure 6.1). Usually, the fungal film will form around the entire circumference of the pathway, blocking it. Or it will form distinct patches in damaged pits and tears that already exist in the lung (such as those caused by tuberculosis or pneumonia). In both situations, the fungi feed at first off the extra mucous the lungs' cells produce to try and flush the invader away. As the infection progresses, the fungi kill these cells. More importantly, they destroy the hair-like cilia these cells use to push the extra mucous out of the lung for disposal in the acidic stomach. The excess mucous begins to clog up the airways in the lungs and to provide even more food for the fungi. Eventually, as the fungi use the dead cells and mucous for nutrition and to reproduce, their hyphae begin to invade through the bronchial wall. The fungi make it into the blood stream where individual cells of the biofilm break off and travel through the body. They spread to the brain, bone, and skin, and once there, start new biofilms which interfere with the normal function of these organs, too.

Because *A. fumigatus* and *A. flavus* attack the lining of the lungs, the initial symptoms of aspergillosis are those of any respiratory infection. Patients develop a flu-like fever and cough, and they often complain of chest pains. As a result, the disease is seldom correctly diagnosed at first, if at all. It is not until the hyphae invade the circulatory system that a doctor may begin to suspect something else is wrong. When the fungus enters the blood, the lungs start to bleed and the blood begins to appear in the saliva and mucous the patient coughs up. These new symptoms tell a doctor that a patient definitely does not have a flu or cold. But because bacterial pneumonia can also cause bleeding in the lungs and blood in the mucous, a doctor may still not correctly diagnose the condition. Aspergillosis remains severely under-diagnosed for this very reason. Often, medical officials do not make a correct diagnosis until after death, when an **autopsy** or **biopsy** reveals through

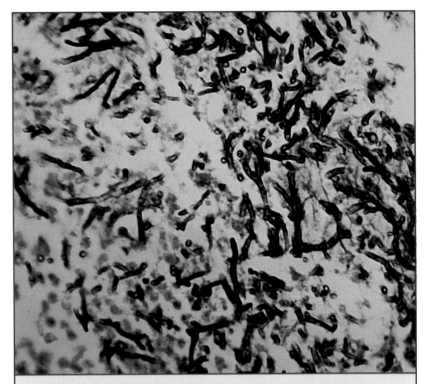

Figure 6.1 This micrograph (magnified 100 times) of a lung sample from a patient with aspergillosis shows the classic symptoms of a fungal biofilm. The hyphae (the dark lines on the right) display the interconnecting cells of the surface of the biofilm, while the hyphae extending into the left of the photo show how the fungus burrows into the lung tissue to seek nutrient resources.

the microscope the true identity of the invader. Of course, by then, it is too late.

And it is almost always "too late." Even when given one of the most powerful antifungal medications of all, **amphotericin B** (see Chapter 8), for as much as *19 days!*, few patients survive an encounter with *A. fumigatus* or *A. flavus* whose immune systems could not already stop the disease. Mortality rates for aspergillosis are often 94%, and with odds like that—to paraphrase an old cliche—"who needs enemies?"

CRYPTOCOCCOSIS

Cryptococcus neoformans is a common yeast found everywhere in the world. Normally a simple saprobe, it lives in the soil decomposing various animal matter and releasing excess nutrients back into the environment. Hence, we might assume that like *A. fumigatus* and *A. flavus,* this yeast simply enters

FOOD POISONING

Fungi don't just infect, they can also poison. *Aspergillis* molds are often the culprit, but toxic fungi can include mushrooms, mildews, and even rusts. In most cases, the fungi produce poisons as **secondary metabolites**. These are chemicals that the fungi don't actually need to survive but which often help them defend themselves from competing microbes. Almost all fresh grains, fruits, and vegetables have some small amount of these toxins coating their surface, and all the washing or cooking in the world cannot get rid of them. But the quantity is usually *so* low that only people who are allergic to these chemicals ever have any kind of reaction. However, when foods start to rot, the concentration of the poisons can get quite high. In places where poverty forces people to eat food in this condition, there is real risk for harm. These poisons have been known to cause liver damage and certain forms of cancer.

Since eating rotting food is not a problem for most of us, the real concern we should have about food poisoning comes from mushrooms. Don't ever eat a mushroom you did not purchase from the grocery. It takes an expert to know which mushrooms in the wild are safe and which are not, and even they sometimes get it wrong. Nausea, vomiting, hallucination, diarrhea, muscle spasms, headache, and even death can result from eating the wrong mushroom. Stick to the professionally grown and harvested ones—they taste great, they're nutritional, and you won't spend your night in the bathroom.

through the lungs from disturbed soil, where it would produce similar symptoms.

But *C. neoformans* has a unique physical feature that makes it slightly different from the other pathogenic fungi in this chapter. Each cell of this yeast encases itself in a tough protective capsule made up of acidic starch molecules. None of the other infectious fungi have this acidic layer as part of their spore, making *C. neoformans* unique from the others in three important ways. First, because of the acidic layer, this fungus can infect people who do not have weakened or stressed immune system. The acidic molecules alter the pH of the blood, hindering the metabolism of the immune cells and slowing down their ability to attack the fungus' cells. Hence, *C. neoformans* is the only opportunistic fungus which can occasionally make healthy people sick, too. Second, the acidic layer prevents the fungus from transforming into a form which can generate a biofilm. As a consequence, its pathology as we shall see is quite different. Third, it enables the disease to spread and to infect people via a carrier rather than only through direct contact with soil. Therefore, cryptococcosis is easier to catch because there are more ways to come into contact with it.

The carriers in question turn out to be birds—especially pigeons—and it is worth taking a moment to explore why. Because birds do not have teeth, they have had to evolve another method for "chewing" their food to grind it up. What they do is eat small bits of earth and tiny stones to store in an organ called the "gizzard." Here, the stones act just like the millstones people use to grind wheat into flour. Any food a bird eats gets mixed with the hard minerals from the dirt which then mash the food into digestible pulp. But along with the bits of rock found in the soil, the birds are obviously consuming the microbes living there as well. Their digestive juices kill most of these. But the acidic layer of *C. neoformans* protects it, and the yeast flourish on the food remnants. As a result, the fungus gets concentrated in a bird's feces, making bird droppings the number one source for this disease.

Mere contact with bird droppings, however, does not automatically produce cryptococcosis. A person does have to inhale the spores, and the spores have to survive long enough to infect. In healthy individuals, only between 0.4 and 1.3 out of 100,000 people who come into contact with the yeast contract the condition annually. This number is much higher among AIDS victims where between 2 and 7 out of every 1,000 patients gets the disease. But even in these individuals, the disease does not begin to attack the body as severely as aspergillosis can. Consequently, cryptococcosis only has a 12% mortality rate.

Unlike other opportunistic fungi, *C. neoformans* produces almost no symptoms of any kind while in the lungs. It is not until the yeast makes it through the blood barrier and into the central nervous system that the patient begins to feel its effects. Once inside the spinal column, the fungus attacks the **meninges**, the tough layer of membranes protecting the spinal cord and the brain. Its outside acidic layer alters the pH of the spinal column's environment, inhibiting the cells there from metabolizing correctly, and then the fungus bombards the body's cells with digestive enzymes to feed itself, killing off the meninges, causing **meningitis**. As it reproduces and spreads, the fungus eventually penetrates into the nerve tissue of the spinal cord and brain. There, it can kill off whole chunks of the central nervous system (Figure 6.2). Brain abscesses and permanent neurological damage are common even when treated in time.

Medical science has only a couple of "advantages" over cryptococcosis that it does not have over the other opportunistic infections. But they are important ones. The first advantage is that meningitis, unlike flu-like diseases, comes on rapidly and has very limited causes. The bacterial form of it responds within a day or two to treatment. The viral form produces

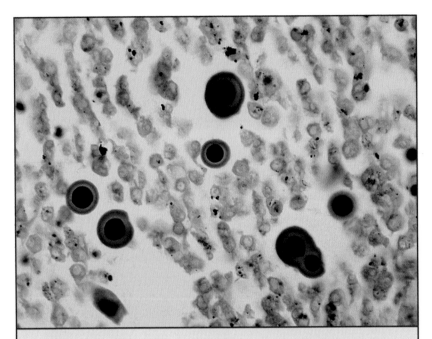

Figure 6.2 *C. neoformans* has a different pathology from the rest of the opportunistic fungi. Here, one of the encapsulated yeast (dark circles with light rings around them) is budding. These budding yeast will use the acidic capsule layer on the outside (the light rings) to kill lung cells for food. Note the cleared areas around each yeast cell on the microscope picture where this process has already happened. The cells in this micrograph have been magnified 160 times.

slightly different symptoms. Thus, the fungal form gets diagnosed with a higher rate of accuracy than other opportunistic fungus infections. This allows for proper treatment to begin sooner. Furthermore, because the encapsulated yeast cannot form a biofilm, medicines can attack it more directly. It is therefore easier to kill, and even in the 7% to 10% of AIDS patients who catch this form of meningitis, there is a relatively high rate of recovery. Again, though, recovery does not mean undamaged. Most people who suffer from this leading cause of fungal meningitis do not come out of it unscathed. Permanent speech impediments and loss of coordinated muscle control are not uncommon.

PNEUMOCYSTOSIS

Formally known as *Pneumocystis carinii* pneumonia (and more commonly as **PCP**), this disease was once the leading killer of AIDS patients. Even today, it remains the single disease most associated with AIDS, and over 75% of people with it contract a case of PCP at some point during their infection. However, the development of more effective **anti-retroviral** drugs in the 1990s that slow the spread of the AIDS virus in the body has reduced the fatality rates from PCP in the North America and Europe dramatically. PCP remains a major

DON'T FEED THE BIRDS

Many people like to sit in the park and throw birdseed or left-over breadcrumbs to the birds. However, in some major urban areas this habit could prove problematic. Pigeons are among the dirtiest animals on earth, and the yeast *C. neoformans* lives in huge quantities in their droppings. This is the same yeast that is the leading cause of fungal meningitis in the world. So where there are many pigeons, the risk of infection can increase by as much as 15%.

This percentage is enough of a risk to trouble the health officials in some of the world's largest cities. For example, perhaps nowhere in the world are there as many pigeons as in Trafalgar Square in London, and the authorities there are in a bit of a quandary right now. The pigeons bring in tourists. But the huge numbers of birds produce droppings faster than the authorities can clean. Hence, much of the Square is constantly covered in potentially hazardous waste. The health officials want the pigeons gone, businesses want them to stay, and no one really knows just how dangerous all that pigeon waste really is.

problem in the developing world, but with fewer cases in the industrial world, it has seceded its position as the number one killer of AIDS victims to aspergillosis.

At one time, medical science believed the causative agent of PCP, *P. carinii*, was actually a **protozoan** and not a fungus. But the most recent consensus is that in spite of being the only single fungus antibiotics can kill (one of the reasons scientists originally assumed it must be a protozoan), *P. carinii* is in fact a member of the fungal kingdom after all. It lives throughout environments worldwide, and victims inhale it into their lungs.

Interestingly, we also now know that *P. carinii* may colonize any lung tissue with which it comes into contact. Genetic analysis of swabbings from the lungs of healthy individuals has found the DNA of this fungus present, and medical scientists now believe that many people contract mild cases of the disease. They think the reason those infected do not experience any symptoms is because their healthy immune systems prevent the fungus from causing a full blown case of PCP.

Sufferers of this disease typically are the immunocompromised, but the first clinical diagnosis of PCP occurred in orphanages in Europe during World War Two where malnutrition was prevalent. Only later in the 1950s did doctors identify cases among cancer patients and others with weakened immune responses. Modern medicine has come to realize that individuals whose diets do not have enough protein in them are also at higher risk for catching PCP, and in areas where malnourishment is widespread, cases of the disease among otherwise healthy people are more common than medical science originally believed.

Regardless of what put someone at risk for infection, when a person does catch PCP, the symptoms are the traditional ones associated with any case of **pneumonia**. The fungus first forms a biofilm inside the lung's **alveoli**, the small air sacs where gas exchange occurs (Figure 6.3). One of the

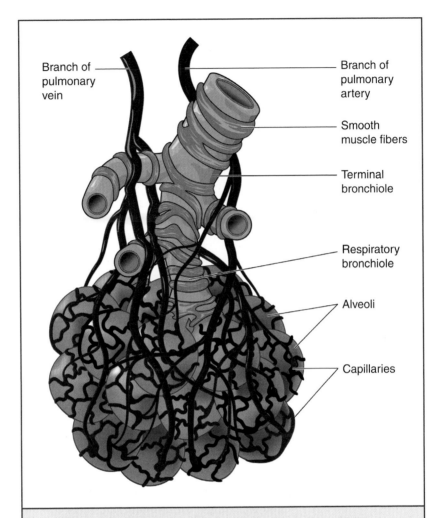

Branch of
pulmonary
vein

Branch of
pulmonary
artery

Smooth
muscle fibers

Terminal
bronchiole

Respiratory
bronchiole

Alveoli

Capillaries

Figure 6.3 The lung's smallest structures are the alveoli. Capillaries of blood surround these tiny, balloon-like sacks, and both the capillary and alveolus walls are so thin that gases in the air and the blood can diffuse through them. Thus, in healthy alveoli, oxygen brought inside during inhalation moves through the walls of the alveoli and capillaries into the bloodstream and carbon dioxide can diffuse out of the lungs for exhalation. When *P. carinii* invades, the alveoli become clogged with fungus and mucus, physically blocking the two gases from diffusing and preventing normal gas exchange in the body.

ways the body then tries to fight the infection is by producing extra mucus to wash the fungus off and make it more accessible to attacking white blood cells. As the fungus spreads, the body produces more and more mucus until the lung actually starts to clog up its own passageways. The patient starts to experience a shortness of breath as the mucus and fungus prevent the exchange of gases between the air and the blood. He or she also starts to cough constantly, trying to expel the excess mucus, and most patients also experience a fever. In extremely severe cases, chest pain and blood in the **sputum** are possible. If left untreated, people suffering from the disease will eventually quite literally drown in their own mucus. The liquid fills up their lungs and the body cannot exchange enough oxygen and carbon dioxide to stay alive.

Diagnosis of pneumonia in general is easy, and it is easily confirmed with an x-ray of the lungs. But to confirm that a patient has PCP, a doctor must identify the presence of the fungus in samples of the patient's sputum or mucus using a microscope. The doctor will then use antibiotics to treat the disease, and in 80% of the patients, treatment is effective. However, because of the severity of the damage *P. carinii* causes, many doctors have often automatically prescribed an antibiotic regimen for high risk patients such as AIDS sufferers without confirming that the patient indeed has PCP. As a result (as we shall see next in this chapter), this potential misuse of antibiotics has had the unintended and unfortunate side-effect of actually increasing an immunocompromised patient's risk for catching candidemia.

CANDIDEMIA

While the other opportunistic fungi invade the body through the lungs, now and then our "friend" from Chapter 3, *C. albicans* and its relatives, can penetrate the body's digestive system, invade the blood stream, and produce a systemic infection. This condition, known as candidemia, is actually the fourth most common blood disease in hospital patients. In 8 out of 100,000 immunocompromised patients, those already suffering from a yeast infection will have that infection develop into full blown candidemia. Cancer patients are particularly vulnerable, and C. albicans is the leading cause of invasive fungal infections in these individuals.

Basically, anything that weakens the body's natural barriers can set up a person for an invasive yeast infection. Surgery, burns, catheters, HIV, antibiotics—they all damage the normal defenses the body uses to protect itself. But oral antibiotics are what really set the stage among the immunocompromised for further infection. These drugs kill off the normal, healthy bacteria which inhabit the gastrointestinal tract. That makes it easier, though, for C. albicans and company to reproduce and colonize larger portions of the digestive system. To make things worse, the immunocompromised need a carbohydrate rich diet to give them the energy to heal in their weakened condition. All those carbohydrates give the yeast extra food *they* can use instead. Thus, between the decreased competition from the bacteria and the increased supply of nutrients, C. albicans can reproduce like crazy. The result is that almost all cases of candidemia start out as thrush infections in the gastrointestinal tract (Figure 6.4).

From there, the fungi use the blood stream as their highway to the rest of the body. They form biofilms first in the blood rich organs such as the kidney, liver, heart, and spleen. Then they can move onto the eyes where they often rupture the retina and cause blindness. If left untreated, the yeast will eventually establish biofilms in the central nervous system, the marrow of the bone, the joints, and the lining of the lungs. At this stage, mortality is around 50%, and even with recovery, the damage to all these critical organs leaves a patient severely endangered. Whatever pathogen attacks next will have an easier time, which is why even if candidemia does not kill someone directly, it often starts them down the path toward death anyway.

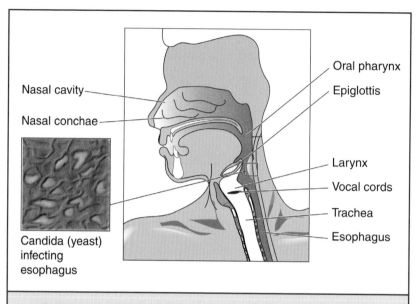

Nasal cavity

Nasal conchae

Candida (yeast)
infecting
esophagus

Oral pharynx

Epiglottis

Larynx

Vocal cords

Trachea

Esophagus

Figure 6.4 Most cases of thrush first appear on the back of the tongue and in the oral pharynx region. In the immunocompromised, *C. albicans* expands into the esophagus where it can more readily penetrate into the blood stream. When this happens, the patient will then develop a case of candidemia.

Part of the problem, of course, is that just like with aspergillosis, this disease's symptoms are so generic. The patient will usually complain only of fever and chills (and once the biofilm on the heart forms, chest pains). But almost every single pathogen known to science causes these. So it is not until antibiotics fail to clear up these symptoms that doctors have a chance to make the correct diagnosis. Once they do, the standard treatment is to deliver amphotericin B or one of the azole drugs (see Chapter 8) intravenously until the symptoms disappear.

The cure, though, as we have regularly mentioned can be worse than the disease. Amphotericin B's nick name is "amphoterrible" for a reason. Hence, prevention continues to remain a central theme in the world of infectious fungi. Most hospitals now know, for instance, that they need to properly maintain invasive tools like catheters and reduce how often they use them. Doing so decreases the likelihood of contracting candidemia a lot. Even more importantly, doctors and nurses now understand the role antibiotics play in catching this disease. They know that excess use and scope of these drugs is what most probably caused the problem in the first place and that changing how we use them can only make things better. Thus, they now know to reduce how often, how long, and how many antibiotics they give immunocompromised patients.

7

The Air We Breathe— Nonopportunistic Fungi

Most of the time when we see a blemish or lesion on our skin, we assume it was something we touched. But sometimes, it comes from something we have inhaled. Take for instance the case of a middle-aged sanitation worker who checked into a New Orleans's hospital in the mid-1990s. For several days, the cheek below his left eye had steadily swollen more and more. It was now severely discolored, riddled with small pock marks and raised nodules. The surgeon treating him sliced open and drained the lesion but was not sure if doing so would cure things or merely fix a symptom. Her diagnosis wavered uncertainly until she learned two things. First, she discovered the gentleman was a pack a day smoker and had been for 30 years. Second, right before the lesion started to grow, the patient had developed a mild and now gently persistent cough. That was the key. She now knew she was not dealing with a typical skin disease. Her patient had North American **blastomycosis** and was being attacked from the inside out. Her patient was fighting a fungus.

GENERAL INFORMATION
The final group of fungi we will explore in this book are those microbes which can infect healthy individuals. Like some of the opportunistic fungi, they gain access to the body through the lungs. But that is where most similarities between these microbes and all the other infectious

fungi ends. For starters, once inside the lungs, they regularly do not produce any symptoms at all. It would take an X-ray to see the minor damage done. Also, unlike the other fungal conditions, the diseases in this category are often native to specific regions. The majority of people who live in these areas become exposed to the specific fungus at some point in their lives. However, for reasons that are unclear, only a small portion of them will have the microbe spread from the lungs to become a systemic infection.

When these illnesses do become systemic, the most common symptoms are not the flu-like ones of the opportunistic fungi (though these can still occur). Instead, these infections regularly appear as skin conditions. This similarity with the tineas can make diagnosis confusing and treatment even more so. Yet both proper diagnosis and treatment are critical. The skin conditions of these fungal infections indicate that the fungus has actually already spread throughout the entire body and is therefore damaging much more than just the skin. It is harming numerous tissues and systems. A doctor, though, who thinks a patient with one of these skin conditions has a tinea will prescribe a topical antifungal medication to apply to the surface of the fungal growth. Topical antifungals cannot address the problem with these diseases because the fungi are not trying to dig in; they are in the process of breaking out. Only oral antifungal drugs can treat the nonopportunistic fungi, and some people have died because of the wrong choice of therapy.

Perhaps the most significant difference between the fungal infections discussed here and in the rest of the book is the general pathology of these organisms. A variety of white soil molds cause all of the types of illnesses. But they usually do so by changing from the mold form into budding yeasts or **spherules**. So instead of forming biofilms like almost all the other infectious fungi, members of this small group act more like parasites. They roam the surface of tissues they invade, killing and eating cells without the orderly pattern of a biofilm. As a result, these fungi are much easier to assault with medicines. Survival rates among patients with even extreme cases is the highest of all the invasive fungal infections. But the mirror image of easier treatment is that the diseases in this chapter are much more likely to recur as well. Like any microbe, these fungi experience **mutations** in their genetic information with each cycle of reproduction. Hence, with each exposure, a person runs the risk of contracting one of these conditions again because the body's immune system may not have seen that specific variation of the fungus. Multiple bouts for individuals who have moved past the **asymptomatic** stage are common.

VALLEY FEVER

Truly a native of the Western hemisphere, *Coccidioides immitis* lives in the soils of the semi-arid regions of the Americas. While its range extends into the countries of Columbia, Ecuador, and Peru, its main area of infectious activity is the southwestern United States and northern Mexico (Figure 7.1). In Arizona, for example, 15 of every 100,000 people suffer from a *C. immitis* infection at some point in their lives. Even many who do not fully contract the disease are still exposed to it, and between 10% and 15% of all Arizona residents test positive for the antibody against it. But the true epicenter for **coccidioidomycosis** is California. In the San Joaquin or Central Valley, infection is **endemic**. Nearly everyone who lives there tests positive for antibodies against the fungus.

The general pathology of the organism is characteristic of the nonopportunistic infectious fungi. Individuals inhale the mold whenever they encounter disturbed soil that has been stirred up into the air. Sixty percent of these people then fail to produce any symptoms at all and never know they have been infected. The remaining 40% will start to show symptoms that can include coughing, fever, chest congestion, skin rashes, and muscle pains. These people will usually heal on

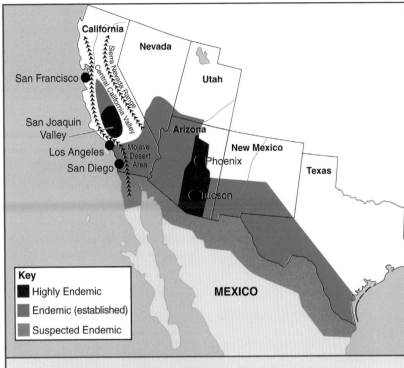

Figure 7.1 *C. immitis* is both indigenous and endemic to the dry, desert climates of the southwestern United States, and the lung disease it causes occurs regularly among the populations who live here. This fungal infection is so prevalent among the farmers and immigrant laborers in California's Central Valley that the common name for the disease is **Valley Fever.** Scientists believe the range of this fungus and its disease extends into the northern desert regions of Mexico, but poor and inadequate medical resources make tracking cases of coccidioidomycosis there difficult.

their own (with or without treatment) because their body's immune systems can fight off the fungus without much difficulty. But for 1% of those who develop symptoms—particularly for unknown reasons among African Americans and pregnant women in their third trimester—the disease will spread into a chronic invasion of the lung tissue. If left untreated, the fungi can produce permanent damage to the lungs and can eventually spread through the blood stream to create a systemic infection. When this happens, the fungi can cause all kinds of damage, ranging from meningitis to deep skin ulcerations and bone lesions.

To prevent this, the 1% who contract a severe case of coccidioidomycosis require the standard regimen of antifungal drugs. But that requires a correct diagnosis. Often in these

FUNGAL SINUSITIS

Imagine one morning you wake up sniffling. "Oh, great," you think, "another cold." But when you go to blow your nose, out come chunks of mushroom! Or at least it looks an awful lot like mushrooms. Suddenly "Oh, great" becomes "OH NO!" You frantically call your doctor. He's never heard of such a thing but offers to see you right away. By this time, you notice that it isn't just the sniffles—you are actually having trouble inhaling and exhaling through your nose. What on earth is happening to you?

Unless you live in northern India or the Sudan, the scenario above is not actually likely to happen to you. But it turns out that your lungs are not the only places in your respiratory system that fungi like to infect. Many molds are just as happy to set up shop in your nasal passages. When they do, the result is fungal sinusitis.

Not all fungal sinusitis clogs up the inside of your nose with "mushrooms." Most cases of the disease just make regular old biofilms and produce a lot of mucus. But certain species can grow and combine their hyphae. When they do, they create branched structures that look a lot like mushrooms. These tend to block your nasal passages, making it hard to breathe. Antifungal medicines can help. But about the only effective treatment is to surgically cut the "mushrooms" out. So the next time you blow your nose and the mucus looks a little unusual, remember: something else could be up there, too.

patients, doctors will initially misdiagnose pneumonia as the cause. But chest x-rays or CT scans can quickly reveal the tell-tale cavities in the lungs. Blood tests can then confirm the presence of antibodies against *C. immitis*, and proper treatment can begin. For those at greater risk, hospitals may also need to culture samples of infected tissue and fluid to see if the fungi are actually there. People who work in construction, farming, and archaeology often already have antibodies from earlier encounters with the fungus. So when members of these professions display the severe symptoms, it is important to determine if an actual fungal infection is present before trying to treat it.

The reason why is that they really might actually have pneumonia or some other illness and need a different type of medication such as an antibiotic. Furthermore, if these patients wrongly use antifungal drugs to treat this other disease that simply has similar symptoms, they run the risk of increasing fungal drug resistance (see Chapter 8). Someday they might actually need those drugs to work. People regularly contract coccidioidomycosis more than once in their lives, and just because they did not show symptoms from their first infection does not mean they will not experience the disease more severely the next time.

HISTOPLASMOSIS

Histoplasmosis is the single most common respiratory fungal infection in the world. Sometimes called "spelunker's disease" because of its association with bats and caves, its causative agent, *Histoplasma capsulatum*, is found everywhere except the polar regions. But the fungus is most endemic in the central and eastern United States (Figure 7.2). It is so common there that 80% percent of the people who live in the Mississippi and Ohio river valleys possess antibodies against this fungus.

A mold often found in bat guano (droppings) and bird droppings (mainly chickens and starlings), it likes to grow in

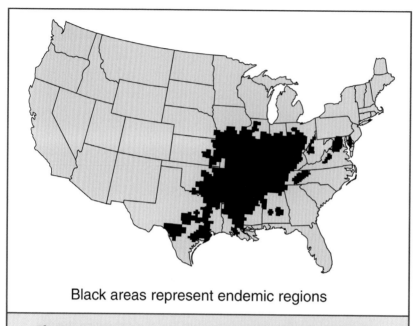

Black areas represent endemic regions

Figure 7.2 The rich moist soil of the watershed of the Mississippi River makes it one of the most fertile agricultural regions in the world. However, it also makes ideal conditions for the fungus *H. capsulatum* to live and grow. The population of the fungus is densest here, making the people who live here more at risk for histoplasmosis than anywhere else in the world.

moist, rich soil. In particular, it likes soils with high levels of nitrogen. This appetite for nitrogen, in turn, reinforces the relationship between birds, bats, and *H. capsulatum*. With birds, they eat the soil with the fungus in it (see Chapter 6). They then excrete nitrogen wastes in their droppings. That, of course, deposits the fungus with more of its food back in the soil where it can use the food to reproduce and increase its population. Thus, the next bird will consume larger amounts of fungi in the dirt it eats, will spread larger amounts of fungi in its droppings, and the cycle repeats. Bats, on the other hand, deposit the guano where they sleep. The drafts of wind from their wings stir up the soil and old dry guano, spreading

H. capsulatum over the fresh food source. The fungi reproduce; the bats produce more guano; their flight stirs up the new fungi; and this cycle repeats as well.

Because of this association with soil, birds, and bats, the mold strikes most often in those people who work with these things. Just like valley fever, construction workers and farmers are the people most at risk of infection because of their regular exposure to stirred up dirt. But individuals in the poultry industry and professional spelunkers are also at risk. Anyone working in any of these fields should use protective breathing masks.

Prevention is vital because when someone does inhale the mold, they run the risk of a life long infection. In the warm, damp environment of the lung, *H. capsulatum* turns into a small budding yeast quite similar to the fungus responsible for cryptococcosis (see Chapter 6). It consumes the cells lining the passageways of the lungs, and in 10% to 25% of infected people, the usual flu-like symptoms appear between three and 17 days later. Correct diagnosis depends on a chest x-ray, and treatment for this acute form employs the usual antifungal therapy.

Yet there is no cure. Following treatment, the yeast persists in the lung for the rest of a person's life. Symptoms can reactivate years later, and over time, permanent lung damage is possible. Furthermore, while it seldom happens, the chronic infection can become a systemic one. In infants, young children, the elderly, and the immunocompromised, *H. capsulatum* can penetrate into the blood stream (Figure 7.3). When that happens, the disease spreads and produces lesions in the spleen, liver, and lymph nodes and creates ulcers in the mouth. Left untreated, this version of histoplasmosis is always fatal.

BLASTOMYCOSIS

Blastomyces dermatitidis is a soil mold endemic to the southern United States and the Midwest but is also found in parts of

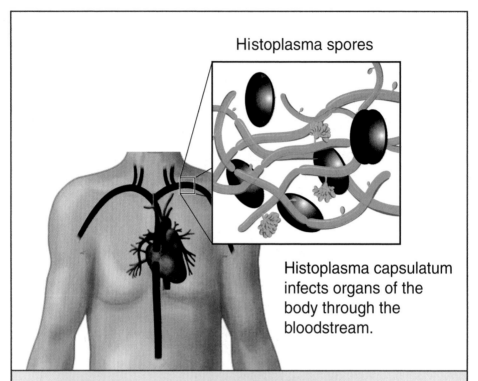

Histoplasma spores

Histoplasma capsulatum infects organs of the body through the bloodstream.

Figure 7.3 *H. capsulatum* rarely invades the bloodstream through the cells lining the inside of the lungs. When it does, however, its spores use the blood as a highway to the rest of the body and colonize in blood-rich organs like the spleen and liver where it attacks their cells and can cause fatal damage.

Africa. It prefers to live in the extremely wet soil of river banks and flood plains. As a result, the major outbreaks of this fungus occur mainly near the Mississippi and Ohio rivers and the Great Lakes region of the United States. (Figure 7.4). One to two out of every 100,000 people living in these areas (or about 0.002% of the total population) contracts the disease at some point in his or her life. Because it is so widespread in this part of the world, the condition is sometimes called "North American blastomycosis." But, again, many cases occur along African waterways as well.

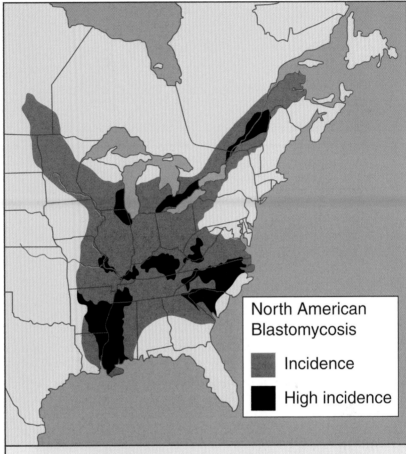

Figure 7.4 Blastomycosis occurs in North America more than anywhere else, mainly in the Ohio, Mississippi, and St. Lawrence River watersheds. The fungus responsible for the disease prefers the moist soil of flood plains and heavily wooded lots found in this part of the world. Over 400,000 of the people who live in the region have caught at least the mild form of the disease at some point in their lives.

Exposure to *B. dermatitidis* happens the same way as all the other fungi of the past two chapters. Disturbed soil, particularly from wooded lots, throws the mold into the air where people inhale it. Once inside the lungs, it turns into a budding yeast. In this case, however, the fungus spreads quickly through the blood stream to the skin (though how quickly varies dramatically from patient to patient and there is no set duration for its dissemination).[1] It *can* produce the usual flu-like

"TO EVERY SEASON..."

Is there anything more annoying than seasonal allergies? For the 20% or more of us who suffer from them every year, seasonal allergies are the bane of our existence. Not only do they cause all those awful symptoms—runny nose, teary eyes, swollen sinuses—but they also cost society hundreds of millions of dollars each year in missed work and medical expenses. Plant pollen is responsible for a lot of them (as that oak tree mistakes the inside of your nose for a flower), but some healthcare professionals believe that the single leading cause of seasonal allergies is actually mold.

More specifically, mold spores. Various kinds of fungi use the spring and summer rains to reproduce, releasing billions of sexual spores into the atmosphere. Wind and weather spread them across the land until one day you have the misfortune to suck some of them up your nose. Once there, the fungi mistake you for the love of their life and basically try to mate. Your body, of course, is not exactly excited by this idea and screams "stop!" It does this by releasing **histamine** and other immune chemicals that cause all those lovely allergy symptoms. You are never in any real danger since the molds aren't trying to infect you. But the stuffy head and burning eyes still aren't any fun.

Interestingly, seasonal allergies don't just affect people. Your pets can have them as well. There are even medicines your cat or dog can take to fight the symptoms. Therefore, if you catch your pet sneezing and wheezing this summer, remember that it might not simply be dust. Some fungus might have decided it has found the ultimate paramour.

symptoms with cough and chest pains. But most often, the lung infection stage manifests nothing. Part of the reason for this is that the immune system regularly stops the disease at this acute stage. Only when *B. dermatitidis* makes it to the skin and forms its lesions (Figure 7.5) do most people become aware of their infection.

Since so many pathogens can infect the skin with similar symptoms, diagnosing blastomycosis correctly poses quite a challenge. In fact, for many years, medical science assumed blastomycosis *was* an infectious skin fungus and that the pathology in the lung was the result of a systemic invasion. But now doctors know that its characteristic skin lesions should lead to an x-ray of the lungs. Any mass that appears tells a doctor that the source of infection is internal rather than external. This information, in turn, should lead a doctor to culture the skin sores for *B. dermatitidis*. Only then can he or she make a correct diagnosis and begin the proper treatment—which, as always, is essential. This fungus can harm an untreated patient significantly. It can cause permanent damage to the lung and lead to bone disintegration and even meningitis without proper therapy. While its systemic version seldom kills (it only has a 5% mortality rate), it can cause lasting disfigurement and life long respiratory problems without the right drugs.

But what are the right drugs? One of the major themes of this book has been the need to match a fungus and its treatment as precisely as possible. Fortunately, those suffering from most cases of blastomycosis can now take one of the oral azoles to cure the disease. However in severe cases and the immunocompromised, doctors must switch therapies and use intravenous amphotericin B.

Why, though, must they switch therapies? This need to change medications returns our attention to a set of questions that have floated around at the end of every chapter. Why do some of the antifungal medicines work on some fungi

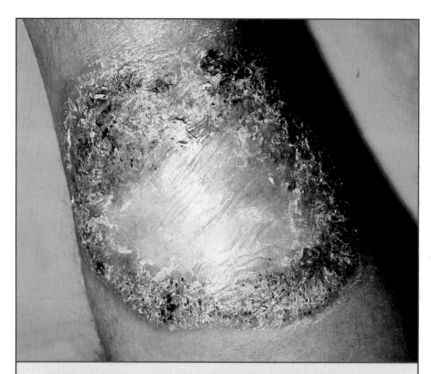

Figure 7.5 Blastomycosis is a disease that affects the internal organs of the body. But it eventually infects so much of the body that populations of the fungus finally colonize the blood vessels near the surface of the skin, and the fungus literally starts to eat its way out, creating lesions like this one. Permanent scarring occurs regularly when the disease reaches this stage.

and not others? Why can they work on one patient and not the next? Why do they have such awful side-effects? Having taken a tour of all the major infectious fungi and their pathologies, it is time to turn our attention to the details of how modern science fights them. In Chapter 8, we will finally look at the antifungal drugs, how they work, and the challenges facing their use.

8

Fighting the Fatal Fungus—Treatment Methods and How They Work

THE CHALLENGES

Modern medicine has made great strides in finding ways to combat the many pathogens that can make people ill. We now have new anti-virals to treat things like the flu, vaccines for chicken pox and mumps, and of course antibiotics for most bacterial infections. However, coping with systemic fungal infections remains a real problem for medical science a lot of the time.

To understand why, let us revisit the discussion in Chapter 1 on why traditional antibiotics do not work on fungi. We already know that antibiotics work on certain organisms because the bacteria and other prokaryotes that attack us have cell structures which are radically different from our own. But what that actually means is that some of the molecules projecting from the surface of a prokaryote are uniquely different from the ones found on the outside of our cells (Figure 8.1). Since any particular molecule has its own unique 3-dimensional shape, medical science can use this uniqueness to target drugs against the pathogen which displays it. A specific antibiotic works because its own shape matches up with the shape of one of the molecules of a bacteria. When the drug meets its matching molecule, they bind together, deactivating the prokaryote's molecule. Then, whatever job that molecule does inside the pathogen can no longer happen, killing it or inhibiting its

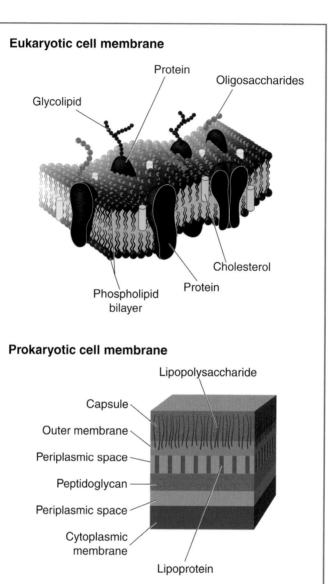

Eukaryotic cell membrane

Protein

Oligosaccharides

Glycolipid

Cholesterol

Phospholipid
bilayer

Protein

Prokaryotic cell membrane

Lipopolysaccharide

Capsule

Outer membrane

Periplasmic space

Peptidoglycan

Periplasmic space

Cytoplasmic
membrane

Lipoprotein

Figure 8.1 These illustrations demonstrate the dramatic differences between the outside membranes of prokaryotes and eukaryotes. In the 2.5 billion years since these categories of cells shared a common ancestor, the molecules protruding from their two membranes have diverged in shape dramatically.

growth. Antibiotics are so successful as a class of drugs because bacteria and other prokaryotes have so many unique molecules our own cells do not have. Thus, when we take these drugs, they do not match the shapes of any of our cells' molecules and so cannot deactivate them (Figure 8.2). Only the pathogen's molecules get deactivated; only it gets killed.

The problem with fungi is that they are eukaryotes just like we are. Their cells have very similar structures to our own. So most of the molecules they project on their surfaces are basically the same as ours (Figure 8.3). As a result, antibiotics do not work against pathogenic fungi. None of these drugs have shapes that match the shape of the fungus' molecules and therefore cannot deactivate them. Without deactivation, though, the molecules still work, keeping the fungus alive.

To kill a fungus, then, medical science needs drugs with shapes that can bind to its molecules. But that presents a real problem. Since both humans and fungi are eukaryotes, we share a lot of molecules in common. A drug that matches the shape of a fungus' molecules will usually match the shape of one of our molecules, too. That means the drug will also deactivate our molecules as well as the fungus'. Hence, it can kill our cells just as easily as it stops the infection.

A treatment that harms its patient is kind of an oxymoron. So medical science has tried to find drugs that will match the shapes of molecules only fungi have. The few molecules found so far appear mainly in the cell wall (a unique structure our cells do not have) and occasionally the cell membrane. But even many of these "unique" fungus molecules still have shapes that are close enough to form a partial fit with our own cells' molecules. **Cross-reactivity** between the antifungal drugs and a patient's own body is quite common. Thus, the high toxicity of these drugs remains an on going problem for modern medicine.

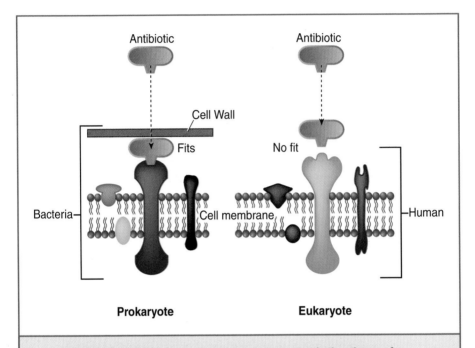

Figure 8.2 The shape of any drug must match the shape of the molecule it attaches to and deactivates or destroys. As the diagrams illustrate, antibiotics are useful for treating infections because they match the shapes of bacteria molecules without matching the shapes of any of our molecules. Thus, they can kill or inhibit bacteria without harming us when we take them.

In addition to cross-reactivity, the other major challenge facing antifungal therapies is the fact that most fungi infect by creating a biofilm. As discussed in Chapter 2, this makes attacking the infection harder because even while a drug kills off one layer of fungus cells, the other layers continue to reproduce and feed off the body. Fighting the infection becomes almost like fighting the mythical hydra of Greek lore: kill one fungus cell and two replace it. The consequence is that doctors must use large amounts of an antifungal drug to try and kill the layers of the biofilm faster than the remaining layers can replace it.

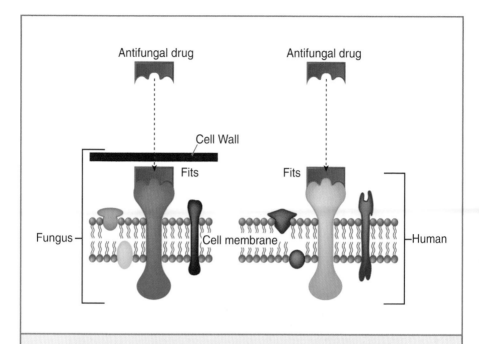

Figure 8.3 Antifungal medications often have unpleasant and toxic side-effects because their shapes match with the molecules on the outside of our own cells as well as the fungus' cells. Hence, when we take an antifungal medication, it often attaches to and damages critical molecules in our body, causing cells to die and us to fall ill.

But that turns treating a systemic fungal infection into a "catch-22." Because of cross-reactivity, most of the antifungal drugs are highly toxic. Yet, because biofilms are so hard to fight, a patient must take large amounts of this toxic chemical to kill it. So the patient must poison a body that already feels sick. It becomes a question of which is worse: the cure or the disease? It is why early diagnosis and early intervention are so essential. The sooner treatment can begin, the smaller the biofilm will still be. A smaller biofilm means the less medicine the patient will need to take, reducing the toxic side-effects.

What medical science needs, therefore, are two things. It needs more medicines that are more unique to the fungi they treat, and it needs better, more effective diagnosis. The latter basically means more training for doctors in the symptoms of systemic fungal infections. Something that is relatively straightforward to do. The former, however, as we are about to see, may prove more challenging.

ANTIFUNGAL MEDICATIONS

Currently, there are five classes of drugs approved for use in the United States to combat infectious fungi. In addition, researchers have developed two vaccines and are working on others. However, of these various medications, doctors and hospitals use only two of them most of the time: the amphotericins and the azoles. The reason is that drugs in these classes all attack a key molecule called "**ergosterol**" which most fungi possess and we do not.

Amphotericin B is the number one drug of choice against systemic fungal diseases. It binds directly to the ergosterol molecules in the cell membrane and changes the membrane's permeability. This change in permeability then allows different positively charged atoms like potassium ions and sodium ions to move more freely through the membrane (Figure 8.4). As a result, the fungus can no longer maintain the correct concentrations of chemicals it needs to survive, and it dies.

Meanwhile, though, this drug is also binding to the cholesterol molecules on the cell membranes of the patient. Cholesterol is one of the ways our cells control membrane permeability. Thus, amphotericin B binding to cholesterol changes our cells' permeability just like it does the fungus', with the same results. Our cells die right along with the fungus. The severity of this toxicity to our own body can be quite severe. Patients taking it regularly experience fever, chills, low blood pressure,

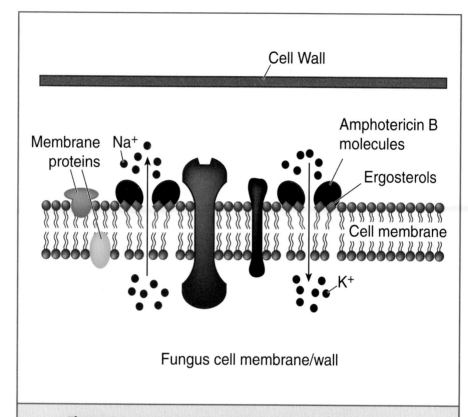

Figure 8.4 Amphotericin B works by attaching to molecules in fungal membranes called ergosterols. When the drug binds to an ergosterol, it creates holes in a fungus' cell membrane that allow two critical ions, Na+ and K+, to flow in and out of these holes. Normally, a cell maintains a low concentration of Na+ on its inside and low K+ on its outside to create an electrical gradient across the two sides of the membrane. Without this gradient, the cell cannot survive. The holes created by the amphotericin B destroy this gradient, killing the cell.

headaches, nausea, inflamed blood vessels, and vomiting—often all at the same time. Kidney damage also regularly occurs because that is where the body concentrates the drug to excrete it. It is easy to see why the drug's nickname among its users is "amphoterrible." But it remains the most effective medication for fighting systemic infectious fungi. Hence, it remains the first drug of choice in many situations.

The other major class of drugs that medicine uses to cure the severe fungal diseases is the azoles. Of them, ketoconazole is the one used the most. It also attacks ergosterol but not directly. Instead, it attacks the biochemical pathway in the cell which makes ergosterol. Fungus cells use enzymes to assemble ergosterol out of smaller molecules known as sterols. Ketoconazole matches the shape of an enzyme with the imposing sounding name, "cytochrome P450 14a-demethylase." When it binds to this enzyme, the cytochrome P450 14a-demethylase cannot make ergosterol out of sterol (Figure 8.5). These precursor molecules then build up in concentration as the cell keeps making them. This growing concentration of sterols creates holes in the fungus' cell membrane. With these holes, the cell cannot prevent vital chemicals and other things from pouring out, and the fungus dies.

Again, however, the full medical picture is not simple. Our bodies also have a collection of cytochrome P450 enzymes. One of the ways we use them is in the liver where they help detoxify harmful chemicals we eat and break down our own metabolic byproducts. Ketoconazole and all the other azoles bind to these cytochrome P450 enzymes just as easily as they do to the one in the fungus. This cross-reactivity means that the azoles have the potential to harm the liver and anywhere else our bodies use these enzymes. It is one of the reasons we mentioned in Chapter 4 that doctors require a blood test before they will prescribe any of these drugs. They have to determine if the liver is healthy enough to cope with the damage the drug will do to it during treatment.

There are other drugs besides amphotericin B and ketoconazole. Some like the fluoropyrimidines block the fungus'

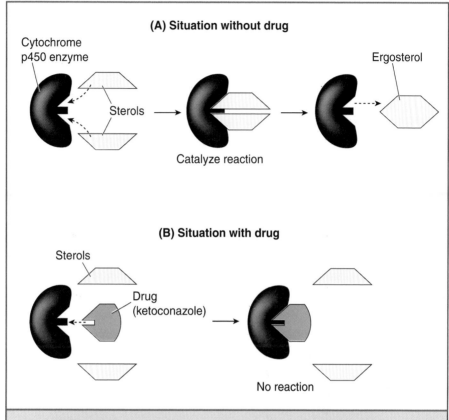

(A) Situation without drug

Cytochrome
p450 enzyme

Ergosterol

Sterols

Catalyze reaction

(B) Situation with drug

Sterols

Drug
(ketoconazole)

No reaction

Figure 8.5 Enzymes like cytochrome P450 are proteins that speed up chemical reaction rates in cells without being destroyed or consumed by the reaction. Each type is responsible for one reaction because only the chemicals that react faster will fit into a particular enzyme's shape. Thus, if another molecule such as ketoconazole has a similar shape that fits into cytochrome P450's shape, it can block out the usual molecules that fit inside the enzyme and stop the reaction from occurring.

ability to make DNA and RNA. Without these critical nucleic acids, the fungus cannot reproduce or manufacture proteins to control its chemical reactions. It dies rapidly. But then our cells die, too, when we take it because we also need DNA and RNA to make our own proteins and replace old cells. Other antifungal medications inhibit the construction of glucan, a vital molecule in the fungus cell wall. When glucan is missing, the cell wall cannot protect the cell membrane and prevent it from rupturing. The fungus dies by slow-motion explosion. The difficulty here is that cells only make lots of glucan when reproducing in order to form a new cell wall. Until then, the fungus can still cause harm. Hence, while there are other drugs besides the amphotericins and azoles, they are not as effective and remain on the periphery of therapy options.

DRUG RESISTANCE

With so few antifungal medicines and even fewer that

THE "FIRST" ANTIBIOTIC

In 1928, the Scottish biologist, Alexander Fleming, was messing around in his lab. Literally. He accidentally contaminated the plates of bacteria he was growing for study. A few days later, he found green mold all over his plates, ruining his experiment. Any other guy would have tossed the plates and started over, but Fleming noticed something very unusual. Everywhere on the plates where the mold came into contact with the bacteria there was an empty zone between the two. He immediately realized that the mold must have released something that killed the bacteria.

That "something" would change the world. Fleming had discovered penicillin, the world's "first" antibiotic. This drug and the others like it revolutionized medicine. Before antibiotics, literally millions of people died each year of bacterial infections, such as tuberculosis. Sore throats could be fatal, and people with persistent coughs lived in fear. Infant and childhood mortality were high. It was not uncommon for only one or two of 10 children in a family to survive to adulthood because of bacterial infections.

are really effective, the greatest challenge to fighting infectious fungi today has become drug resistance. While the problems of cross-reactivity and toxic side-effects are not minor ones, at least in the recent past, the various fungicides have actually helped cure people. But now, more and more fungi can survive these drugs, causing more and more people to die from them. This is particularly true for the *Candida* species. There are strains of *C. albicans* that have acquired enough mutations to survive all the azoles we can throw at them and even some of the amphotericins. Given that this yeast is the number one cause of systemic fungal infections (see Chapter 6), drug resistance like this is no small matter.

Today, numbers like that shock us. We take antibiotics for granted. Very few people ever die anymore of a simple staphylococcal infection. But did you know that antibiotics have actually been around for billions of years? Even penicillin, named after the mold that makes it, *Penicillium*, has been around for millions of years. The reason is because fungi and bacteria have been around for so long. These two groups of microbes have been eating each other and competing against each other for billions of years. What we call antibiotics are simply the chemicals they use to fight and defend themselves against each other.

What this means for science is that fungi are one of the major sources we can harvest for new antibiotics. Billions of years of evolution have provided many possible answers on how to fight a bacterium. All we have to do is look for them. Thus, while Fleming may not really have discovered the first antibiotic, he did show us where to look: our friends, the fungi.

But how does a fungus become resistant to a drug? At the most basic level, the answer is through mutation. Each time a cell copies its genetic material in order to reproduce, it can make small errors. Most of the time, these errors are either fatal or meaningless. Either the new cell dies right away before it can pass on its error to its offspring, or it has no effect. Thus, whether fatal or meaningless, the error has no impact on the fungus or on future generations of it. Sometimes, though, the small error produces a new protein or an old protein with a slightly different shape that can actually help the fungus survive better. Then when the fungus encounters a new situation like exposure to a drug, this error may keep the drug from killing it.

It will also keep any future offspring alive, too. The fungus will pass on this new genetic information each time it reproduces, and its daughter cells will do likewise. All these new cells, however, can also make their own new small errors when copying their DNA. These additional errors will also prove either fatal, meaningless, or useful. If useful, the descendant fungi now have a new protein variation that might help them survive a different drug. Hence, generation after generation, the number of medications a fungus can become resistant to can steadily grow.

In the case of the infectious fungi, the specific mutations we are seeing today mainly involve ergosterol and the proteins of the cell wall (Figure 8.6). *C. albicans*, for instance, can now resist the azoles in four different ways. Some cells can produce more proteins to pump the drug out of the cell. Others have changed the shape of the cytochrome P450 enzyme so that the drug's shape no longer matches up, and it can no longer bind to it. Still others now create so many extra quantities of this enzyme that even when azole binds to one, there are too many other copies of the enzyme present that can still make ergosterol. Finally, a few strains of *C. albicans* have simply started producing a different variation of ergosterol.

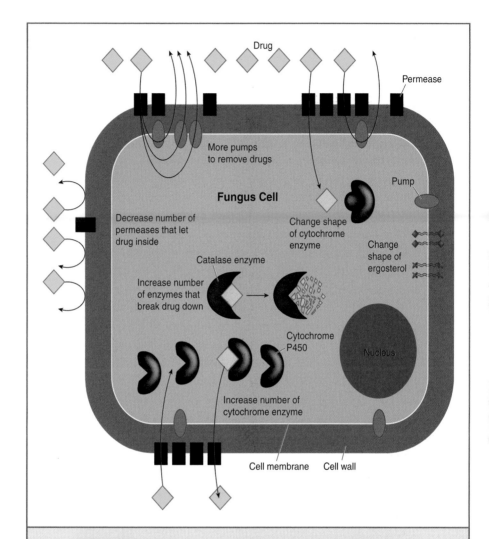

Figure 8.6 Infectious fungi have evolved six unique ways to resist antifungal drugs by: (1, 2) changing the shape of ergosterol or cytochrome P450 so the drugs no longer can bind to them; (3) producing extra copies of cytochrome P450, making the concentration of the drug lethal to the patient; (4) decreasing the production of permease proteins in cell membranes so fewer drugs can get inside; (5) producing more protein pumps in their membranes to remove the drug as it enters; and (6) creating more catalytic enzymes to break the drug down faster once it enters.

WHAT YOU DON'T KNOW, *CAN* KILL YOU

Modern medicine is facing a real crisis. More and more, the drugs we have always used to treat microbial infections aren't working. Antibiotics, fungicides, and parasitic prophylactics lose effectiveness because bacteria, fungi, and protozoa grow more resistant to them every day. There are actually some strains of bacteria that are now resistant to every antibiotic we have. We literally can't kill them using just simple drugs.

The basic process of natural selection is the culprit behind this phenomenon. Each time an antibiotic is taken, it kills most of the infectious bacteria. Or at least it kills enough of them that the immune system can rid the rest. Because of mutations, *some* of those bacteria can resist the drug. They'll live, and because all their neighbors are now dead, they have extra food so they can reproduce freely. However, that means these resistant bacteria will be the only type around. Thus, the next time they infect you, the first kind of antibiotic won't work. Of course, you say you'll just take a different antibiotic next time. But then the process repeats itself, and *now* the bacteria are resistant to *both* drugs.

Similar changes in various fungi also account for the increased resistance to amphotericin B. Certain fungi have altered the shape of ergosterol so that the drug cannot match up and bind with it. Others have increased the number of **catalase** proteins which breakdown and metabolize the drug as it enters the cell. Some have even decreased how much of the drug enters the cell by decreasing the number of **permease** proteins or "doorways" that let the drug inside.

What all of these methods add up to, however, is that infectious fungi of all kinds are becoming harder to fight. With each new kind of resistance, both systemic and non-systemic

To make matters worse, a lot of people don't use antibiotics and other antimicrobials correctly. They don't take the full dose of medicine because they start feeling better before the medication is finished. When that happens, the body has not only stored the surviving resistant microbes but some of the non-resistant microbes as well. And for reasons we still don't fully understand, the resistant ones like to *share* their resistance with their non-resistant cousins. Now, the body not only contains resistant microbes, but also a *lot more* of them. You can see where this is going. We are forcing the evolution of resistant microbes by presenting them with an environmental force (the drug) which selects for survival, and we're not just doing it with our own bodies. Farmers and the commercial food industry pour antibiotics into cattle feed and chicken meal to increase the numbers of livestock that make it to market. We also spray fields and orchards with insecticides to protect against fungal diseases, and every time, the survivors come back stronger.

infections last longer. They do more damage, and they make a patient more prone to the next infection. Proper use of these drugs is critical (see sidebar on pages 104–105). But even more critical is the need for more research and drug development. Like bacteria and viruses, fungi are one of our oldest medical foes. But while the battle never ends, it is up to future doctors and scientists to make sure it is one we do not lose too often.

Glossary

Adhesins—A class of proteins that bacteria, fungi, and algae use to attach and anchor themselves to a surface.

Algae—A group of simple, often microscopic organisms whose cells have a nucleus and which can use photosynthesis to make their own food.

Alveoli—The small grape-shaped air sacks in the lungs where the body exchanges oxygen from the air for carbon dioxide in the body's blood.

Amphotericin B—A drug used to fight fungal infections that works by damaging the cell membrane of fungi.

Antibiotics—Drugs that kill bacteria or slow their rate of reproduction.

Antibodies—Proteins the human immune system makes to fight invading organisms; singular is antibody.

Anti-retroviral—A substance that destroys or inhibits viruses that use RNA as their genetic material instead of DNA.

Antiseptics—Chemicals used to kill microscopic organisms and sterilize a surface like an operating table or a surgeon's skin.

Aspergillosis—A disease of the lungs that can spread to the brain, bone, and skin caused by the fungus *Aspergillis fumigatus* or *A. flavus*.

Asymptomatic—A medical condition in which the illness does not produce any physical or clinical symptoms.

Autopsy—The dissection of a dead human being in order to determine the cause of death.

Azole—A class of drugs used to fight fungal infections that work by interfering with the formation of a key molecule found in the cell membrane of fungi.

Bacterium—A single celled microscopic organism that does not organize its genetic material in a nucleus. Plural is bacteria.

Benign—Not harmful.

Biocides—Chemicals that are toxic to all living things and can be used to sterilize any area or object completely.

Biofilm—A community of microscopic organisms such as bacteria, fungi, or algae that have attached themselves to the surface of a structure by producing chemicals that glue the microbes both to each other and to the surface.

Biopsy—The removal of a tiny piece of tissue from a person to determine if the cells of that tissue are healthy or whether something has diseased the tissue.

Blastomycosis—A disease of the lungs that can spread to the skin caused by the fungus *Blastomyces dermatitidis.*

Budding—A method a yeast can use to reproduce by creating a bulge in its cell wall and membrane and protruding a new cell out of the original one.

Candidiasis—A disease of the digestive tract and the vagina caused by the yeast, *Candida albicans.*

Candidemia—A disease of the bloodstream caused by the yeast, *Candida albicans.*

Catalase—A type of protein cells use to digest and breakdown dangerous chemicals created during normal cell metabolism.

Catheter—A tube inserted into a passageway or cavity in the body to drain fluid.

Chitin—A protein found in the cell walls of fungi which strengthens the walls and makes the cells sturdier. It gives mushrooms their spongy feel. The protein is also in the outside skeleton of insects and is the chemical that makes the outside shell hard.

Chromoblastomycosis—A disease of the skin usually caused when one of the following four fungi enters the skin through a wound (*Cladophialophora carrionii* , *Fonsecaea compacta* or *F. pedrosoi, Phialophora verrucosa*).

Coccidioidomycosis—A disease of the lungs that can spread to the brain, spine, bones, and skin caused by the fungus, *Coccidioides immitis.* Also known as Valley Fever.

Collagen—A protein the human body makes to connect cells together; regularly found in high concentrations in connective tissues such as the ligaments that hold bones together.

Cross-reactivity—When a drug or medication can react with the organism causing a disease and can react with the cells of the patient at the same time.

Cryptococcosis—A disease of the lungs which can spread to the central nervous system caused by the fungus, *Cryptococcus neoformans.*

Cutaneous—Something involving the two outermost layers of cells that make up human skin.

Glossary

Cytoplasm—The collection of proteins, inorganic chemicals, and water that forms the interior space of cells.

Dermatophytes—A group of molds that can attach to the surface of the skin and create rashes and other infections.

Endemic—When something is native or restricted to a specific region.

Epidemic—A situation where the number of cases of a disease in a specific area suddenly increases in a specific but usually relatively short period of time. The size of area and time period can vary from one kind of disease to another as determined by the Centers for Disease Control and the World Health Organization.

Epidermis—The outermost layer of cells of the three layers that make up human skin.

Ergosterol—A molecule found only in the cell membranes of fungi that is derived from cholesterol. It serves as a target for most medicines used against fungi.

Eukaryotes—The group of organisms with cells that organize their genetic material into a nucleus and contain distinct membrane-bound structures that carry out the different cellular activities.

Eukaryotic—Possessing or having cells with a nucleus and distinct membrane-bound structures.

Fauna—Any living species of the animal kingdom.

Fibronectin—A protein the human body uses to connect cells together into tissues and tissues into organs, gives organs like the liver their shape.

Fungicide—A chemical that kills fungi but is not necessarily harmful to other kinds of organisms.

Fungus—A simple, usually microscopic organism whose cells have a nucleus, possesses a cell wall as well as cell membrane, but cannot engage in photosynthesis. It must get its nutrition by consuming other organisms or organic material. Plural is fungi.

Heterotrophs—Organisms that cannot make their own food by photosynthesis and must consume other organisms or organic matter to get their nutrition.

Histamine—A chemical the immune system releases to cause blood vessels to swell and that can make the lining of the nasal passages increase mucus production.

Histoplasmosis—A disease of the lungs that can spread to the spleen, liver, and mouth caused by the fungus, *Histoplasma capsulatum*. Also known as Spelunker's Disease.

Homeostasis—The condition of having a stable internal environment inside of a cell or organism.

Hydrolysis—The chemical process that breaks complex molecules into their simpler building blocks using water.

Hyphae—The finger-like projections and filaments that make up the physical structures of molds and other fungi; used to acquire food and other nutrition.

Immunocompromised—Individuals who have difficulty fighting off diseases because of damaged or weakened immune systems.

Inoculation—The placement of all or part of a microscopic organism or virus into the body; often results in infection or immunity to the organism or virus.

Lesion—An injury or open wound.

Lichens—A group of organisms that are actually made of a fungus and an algae living together in a mutually beneficial and dependent relationship.

Lymphatic system—The collection of vessels and nodes inside the human body which reabsorb and transport liquid lost from the blood to return this fluid back to the blood. Part of the immune system, it also helps clean and filter dead invaders and immune cells out of the blood.

Madura foot—A disease of the skin caused when *Acremonium* molds enter through a wound. Also known as mycetoma.

Meiosis—The process of cell division reproductive cells use to divide the genetic material of an organism in half and produce a sex cell such as egg or sperm containing half the original genetic information for that organism.

Meninges—The tissue layer surrounding the brain and spinal chord that protects them.

Meningitis—The condition when the cells that form the protective layer surrounding the brain and spinal chord become inflamed.

Metabolic pathway—A sequence of chemical reactions living things use to provide energy and resources for their activities.

Glossary

Microbes—The collective term for any and all microscopic organisms.

Mitosis—The process of normal cell division in which a cell duplicates its genetic material and then splits into two new cells, each containing a full copy of the original cell's genetic information.

Monomers—The smaller molecules which cells join together to build their more complex molecules.

Morphogenesis—The process when a living thing organizes its physical structures or rearranges them to produce a new form.

Mutation—A change in the genetic information of an organism that can result in the production of a new protein or a different version of an existing protein. This change can affect how the organism looks or what it is able to do.

Mycetoma—A disease of the skin caused when *Acremonium* molds enter through a wound. Also known as Madura foot.

Mycorrhizae—Plant roots that have soil fungi living as part of them in a mutually beneficial and dependent relationship between the plant and the fungus.

Mycoses—General term for diseases caused by fungi. An individual fungus infection is a mycosis.

Nosocomial—An infection, disease, or illness that a patient catches as a result of being in the hospital for something else.

Oncology—The study and treatment of cancer.

OPC—A disease of the mouth and esophogus caused by candida yeast; also known as oropharyngeal candidiasis or thrush.

Opportunistic fungi—The group of fungi that can only infect a person with a damaged or weakened immune system.

Opportunistic infection—An illness that occurs because a damaged or weakened immune system cannot fight off the invading organism the way a healthy immune system would automatically do.

Oropharyngeal candidiasis—A disease of the mouth and esophagus caused by *Candida* yeast; also known as OPC or thrush.

Pandemic—A disease that has spread so fast and to so many people that huge numbers of cases are found everywhere around the world; a worldwide epidemic.

Parasitic—Living off of another organism at the expense of that other organism's health.

Pathogen—An organism or virus that can make a person sick.

Pathology—The study of disease; also the sequence of events and symptoms a disease produces during an illness.

PCP—The abbreviation for *Pneumocystis carinii* pneumonia, a disease of the lungs caused by this fungus that is commonly associated with AIDS.

Permease—A type of protein found in the cell membrane that helps transport materials through the membrane without using energy. They act like doors and windows into the cell.

***Pneumocystis carinii* pneumonia**—A disease of the lungs caused by this fungus that is commonly associated with the disease AIDS.

Pneumocystosis—A disease of the lungs caused by the fungus, *Pneumocystis carinii,* that is commonly associated with the disease AIDS.

Pneumonia—A disease of the lungs in which the body produces excess mucus to fight an infection and the mucus fills up the lungs over time.

Polymers—Large, complex molecules made up of regularly repeating smaller molecules strung together. The smaller molecules have the same relationship to their larger molecule that railroad cars have to the full train.

Prokaryotes—The group of organisms, including bacteria, whose cells have no nucleus or other internal organizing structures. They possess only cell membranes, cell walls, genetic material, and structures to produce proteins.

Protists—A group of usually single-celled organisms that includes protozoa, algae, and slime-molds.

Protozoan—A single cell animal.

Ringworm—One of the diseases caused by one of the *Trichophyton, Microsporum,* or *Epidermophyton* molds, formally known as tinea corpis to distinguish it from the other, related skin disease these molds cause.

Saprobes—Organisms that decompose organic material to get their nutrition; singular "saprobe."

Secondary infection—An illness that develops after an earlier organism has already invaded the body and created the conditions for the second invading organism to thrive where otherwise it could not.

Glossary

Secondary metabolites—Chemicals the cell produces as byproducts during its activities which the cell does not need or use in those activities; commonly released as protective "wastes."

Septa—The wall that separates the filaments of fungi into individual cells, regulating the flow of materials between them; plural is septae.

Spherules—Cells that have a round shape.

Spores—Single celled organisms with a tough, protective protein coat encasing them; often a reproductive cell.

Sporotrichosis—A disease of the skin caused when the mold, *Sporothrix schenckii*, enters through a wound; common among plant nursery and greenhouse workers.

Sputum—The mixture of mucus from the lungs and saliva from the mouth produced when a person coughs.

Squamous cell carcinoma—A type of skin cancer.

Subcutaneous—The bottom, inner most layer of cells of the three layers that make up human skin.

Systemic infection—An illness that has spread throughout the inside of the body, affecting numerous organs and tissues.

Thrush—A disease of the mouth and esophagus caused by *Candida* yeast; also known as oropharyngeal candidiasis or OPC.

Tinea—Any infection of the surface of the skin caused by a variety of *Trichophyton*, *Microsporum*, or *Epidermophyton* molds; uses of the term usually also include the specific location on the body of the infection: tinea corpis (body), tinea capitis (scalp), tinea curis (groin), tinea unguium (nails), tinea pedis (foot).

Tissue—An organized collection of cells which perform a common function together.

Tracheotomy—A medical procedure in which a tube is inserted directly through the skin of the throat and then through the wall of the passageway leading into the lungs to allow someone with a blocked breathing passageway to inhale and exhale.

Valley Fever—A disease of the lungs that can spread to the brain, spine, bones, and skin caused by the fungus, *Coccidioides immitis*. Also known as Coccidioidomycosis.

Vector—Something that carries and delivers an infectious agent from one living host to another.

Virulent—Having the capacity to cause another organism to become ill.

Virus—A microscopic organism consisting of either DNA or RNA surrounded by a protein coat that is metabolically inert; it must highjack the inner machinery of living cells to reproduce itself.

Vulvovaginal candidiasis—A disease of the lining of the vagina and the tissue folds surrounding it caused by *Candida* yeast; also known simply as a yeast infection.

Zygomycosis—A disease of the nasal passages caused by a variety of soil molds that commonly occurs in areas of natural disasters; also known as mucormycosis.

Notes

CHAPTER 1

1   Steve Sternberg, "The emerging fungal threat." *Science* 266, no. 5191 (1994): 1632-1635.

CHAPTER 2

1   J. Peter Donnelly, "An aspirin a day keeps the biofilm at bay." *Infectious Disease Alert* 23, no. 9 (2004): 99-101.

CHAPTER 3

1   Steve Sternberg, "The emerging fungal threat." *Science* 266, no. 5191 (1994): 1632-1635.

CHAPTER 7

1   Jeff Weingardt and Yuk-Pui Li, "North American blastomycosis." *American Family Physician* 43, no. 4 (1991): 1245-1249.

Bibliography

Alberts, B., D. Bray, J. Lewis, et al. *Molecular Biology of the Cell.* New York, NY: Garland Publishing, Inc., 1983.

American Academy of Family Physicians. "Fungal Infections of Fingernails and Toenails." *familydoctor.org.* Available online at http://familydoctor.org.

American Academy of Family Physicians. "Vaginal Yeast Infections." *American Family Physician* 69, no. 9 (2004): NA.

American Academy of Otolaryngology-Head and Neck Surgery. "Fact Sheet: Fungal sinusitis." *AAO-HNS ENT Health Information.* Available online at http://www.entnet.org.

American Osteopathic College of Dermatology. "Fungus Infections: Preventing Recurrence." *Dermatological Disease Database.* Available online at http://www.aocd.org.

Bruce, A. "Fungal Keratitis; (keratomycosis)." *Optician* (2002): 1.

Buckley, D., L. C. Fuller, E. Higgins, A. du Vivier. "Tinea Capitis in Adults." *British Medical Journal* 320, no. 7246 (2000): 1389.

Calderon, Richard. "Candida." *AccessScience@McGraw-Hill.* Available online at http://www.accessscience.com.

Campbell, N., J. Reece. *Biology,* 6th ed. San Francisco, CA: Benjamin Cummings, 2002.

Center for Disease Control. "Mycotic Disease Listing." *Division of Bacterial and Mycotic Diseases: Mycotic Diseases Branch.* Available online at http://www.cdc.gov/ncidod/dbmd/mdb/diseases.htm.

"Chromoblastomycosis." *DermNet NZs.* Available online at http://www.dermnetnz.org/fungal/chromoblastomycosis.html

"Chromoblastomycosis." *Doctor Fungus.* Available online at http://www.doctorfungus.org/mycoses/human/other/chromoblastomycosis.htm

"Chromoblastomycosis." *The University of Adelaide: Mycology Online.* Available online at http://www.mycology.adelaide.edu.au/mycoses/subcutaneous/chromoblastomycosis.htm

Clarke, A., J. Skelton, R. Fraser. "Fungal Tracheobronchitis: Report of 9 Cases and Review of the Literature." *Medicine* 70, no. 1 (1991): 1–14.

Dickerson, Louise. "Mycotoxin." *Gale Encyclopedia of Science,* 3rd edition. Ed. K. Lee Lerner and B. W. Lerner. Detroit, MI: Gale, 2004.

Bibliography

Donnelly, J.P. "An Aspirin a Day Keeps the Biofilm at Bay." *Infectious Disease Alert* 23, no. 9 (2004): 99-101.

Fincher, R. M., J. Fisher, R. Lovell, et al. "Infection Due to the Fungus *Acremonium (Cephalosporium)*." *Medicine* 70, no. 6 (1991): 398-410.

Flappan, S. M., J. Portnoy, P. Jones, C. Barnes. "Infant Pulmonary Hemorrhage in a Suburban Home with Water Damage and Mold (*Stachybotrys atra*)." *Environmental Health Perspective* 107, no. 11 (1999): 927-930.

Forbes, D, L. Ee, P. Camer-Pesci, P.B. Ward. "Fecal Candida and Diarrhea." *Archives of Disease in Childhood* 84, no. 4 (2001): 328.

Frey, Rebecca. "Vulvovaginitis." *Gale Encyclopedia of Medicine*, 2nd edition. Ed. J. L. Longe and D. S. Blanchfield. Detroit, MI: Gale, 2002.

Haggerty, M. "Ringworm." *Gale Encyclopedia of Medicine*, 2nd edition. Ed. J. L. Longe and D. S. Blanchfield. Detroit, MI: Gale, 2002.

Halde, C., J. P. Woods. "Medical Mycology." *AccessScience@McGraw-Hill*. Available online at http://www.accessscience.com.

Harder, T. "Research interests and previous projects of Dr. Tilmann Harder." *Institute for Chemistry and Biology of the Marine Environment*. Available online at http://www.icbm.de/~harder/8147.html.

Haron, E., S. Vartivarian, E. Annaisse, et al. "Primary *Candida* Pneumonia: Experience at a Large Cancer Center and Review of the Literature." *Medicine* 72, no. 3 (1993): 137-143.

Helweg-Larsen, J. "S-adenosylmethionine in Plasma to Test for *Pneumocystis Carinii* Pneumonia." *The Lancet* 361, no. 9365 (2003): 1237.

Johnston, N. "Debaffling Biofilms: Studies Follow Transformations and Detail a Major Signal." *The Scientist* 18, no. 15 (2004): 34-35.

Jones, C. "Pneumocystis Pneumonia." *Gale Encyclopedia of Medicine*, 2nd edition. Ed. J. L. Longe and D. S. Blanchfield. Detroit, MI: Gale, 2002.

Kaiser, L., T. Huguenin, P. D. Lew, et al. "Invasive Aspergillosis: Clinical Features of 35 Proven Cases at a Single Institution." *Medicine* 77, no. 3 (1998): 188-195.

Kobayashi, G. "Fungal Infections." *AccessScience@McGraw-Hill*. Available online at http://www.accessscience.com.

Kontoyiannis, D., R. Lewis. "Antifungal Drug Resistance of Pathogenic Fungi." *The Lancet* 359, no. 9312 (2002): 1135.

Lampert, R. "Candidiasis." *Gale Encyclopedia of Medicine*, 2nd edition. Ed. J. L. Longe and D. S. Blanchfield. Detroit, MI: Gale, 2002.

Lefferts, L., S. Schmidt. "Molds: The Fungus among Us." *Nutrition Action Healthletter* 18, no. 9 (1991): 1-5.

Lerner, K. L., B. Wilmoth Lerner. *World of Microbiology and Immunology*. Detroit, MI: Gale, 2003.

"Madura Foot." *Encyclopedia Britannica*. Available online at http://search.eb.com/eb/article?tocid=9049930.

Mayo Foundation for Medical Education and Research. "Valley Fever." *MayoClinic.com*. Available online at http://mayoclinci.com.

McGinnis, M. R. "Chromoblastomycosis and Phaeohyphomycosis: New Concepts, Diagnosis, and Mycology." *Journal of the American Academy of Dermatology* 8 (1983):1-16.

McVeigh, G. "6 Steps to Erase Nail Fungus—for Good!" *Prevention* 42, no. 7 (1990): 54-59.

Mitchell, S. J., J. Gray, M. E. I. Morgan, M. D. Hocking, G. M. Durbin. "Nosocomial Infection with *Rhizopus microsporus* in Preterm Infants: Association with Wooden Tongue Depressors." *The Lancet* 348, no. 9025 (1996): 441-444.

Morris, A., J. Lundgren, H. Masur, et al. "Current Epidemiology of Pneumocystis Pneumonia." *Emerging Infectious Diseases* 10, no. 10 (2004): 1713-1721.

Nardi, J. B. *The World Beneath Our Feet: A Guide to Life in the Soil*. New York, NY: Oxford University Press, 2003.

National Library of Medicine at the National Institutes of Health. Available online at http://www.nlm.nih.gov.

Norvell, L. "Fungi." *Biology*, ed. R. Robinson. New York, NY: Macmillan, 2002.

Radentz, W. "Fungal Skin Infections Associated with Animal Contact." *American Family Physician* 43, no. 4 (1991): 1253-1257.

Stern, K. R. *Introductory Plant Biology*, 5th ed. Dubuque, IA: Wm. C. Brown Publishers, 1991.

Bibliography

Sternberg, S. "The Emerging Fungal Threat." *Science* 266, no. 5191 (1994): 1632-1635.

Tasci, S, S. Ewig, A. Burghard, B. Ludertiz. "Pneumocystis Carinii Pneumonia (Case Report)." *The Lancet* 362, no. 9378 (2003): 124.

Weingardt, J., and Y. P. Li. "North American Blastomycosis." *American Family Physician* 43, no. 4 (1991): 1245-1249.

Further Reading

Dermatology Image Atlas. Available online at http://dermatlas.med.jhmi.edu/derm.

Doctor Fungus. Available online at http://www.doctorfungus.org.

Gale Encyclopedia of Medicine, 2nd edition. Ed. Jacqueline L. Longe and Deirdre S. Blanchfield. Detroit, MI: Gale, 2002.

Lerner, K. Lee, Brenda Wilmoth Lerner. *World of Microbiology and Immunology.* Detroit, MI: Gale, 2003.

Nardi, James B. *The World Beneath Our Feet: a Guide to Life in the Soil.* New York, NY: Oxford University Press, 2003.

National Center for Infectious Diseases. "Division of Bacterial and Mycotic Diseases." *Center for Disease Control.* Available online at http://www.cdc.gov/ncidod/dbmd.

National Library of Medicine at the National Institutes of Health. Available online at http://www.nlm.nih.gov.

Valley Fever Center For Excellence. Available online at http://www.vfce.arizona.edu.

Index

Index

Index

Picture Credits

11: © Peter Lamb, HFS Imaging
12: © Simko/Visuals Unlimited
13: Scherer Illustration
21: © Peter Lamb, HFS Imaging
23: © Peter Lamb, HFS Imaging
23: © Dr. Dennis Kunkel/Visuals Unlimited
26: © Peter Lamb, HFS Imaging
27: © Peter Lamb, HFS Imaging
33: © Mediscan/Visuals Unlimited
36: © Peter Lamb, HFS Imaging
36: © Dr. David Phillips/Visuals Unlimited
44: © Dr. Ken Greer/Visuals Unlimited
45: © Dr. Everett S. Beneke/Visuals Unlimited
46: Courtesy PHIL, CDC
47: © Dr. Ken Greer/Visuals Unlimited
54: © Everett Beneke/Visuals Unlimited
55: © Peter Lamb, HFS Imaging

57: © Dr. Ken Greer/Visuals Unlimited
66: © Dr. Arthur Siegelman/Visuals Unlimited
70: © Dr. Gladden Willis/Visuals Unlimited
73: © Peter Lamb, HFS Imaging
76: © Peter Lamb, HFS Imaging
81: © Peter Lamb, HFS Imaging
84: © Peter Lamb, HFS Imaging
86: © Peter Lamb, HFS Imaging
87: © Peter Lamb, HFS Imaging
90: © Dr. Ken Greer/Visuals Unlimited
92: © Peter Lamb, HFS Imaging
94: © Peter Lamb, HFS Imaging
95: © Peter Lamb, HFS Imaging
97: © Peter Lamb, HFS Imaging
99: © Peter Lamb, HFS Imaging
103: © Peter Lamb, HFS Imaging

Cover: © Dr. Dennis Kunkel/Visuals Unlimited

About the Author

David Brock is a veteran, nationally acclaimed science educator with over 16 years of experience. A 2001 Presidential Awardee, he currently teaches at Roland Park Country School in Baltimore, Maryland. He is the project director for the Environmental Science Summer Research for Young Women and has received numerous grants from the Toshiba America Foundation and other organizations for his work with adolescent girls and soil ecology. He has worked on microbe education at the Marine Biological Lab and the Paul F-Brandwein Institute, and he regularly gives workshops on how to study soil microbes in the classroom. In 2002, his soil ecology curriculum for high schools students earned the Gustav Ohaus Award from the National Science Teachers Association, and in 2005, they identified this program as one of 15 exemplary science teaching programs in the country. He has published over 60 articles, book chapters, and reviews in such journals as *The American Biology Teacher*, *Science Activities*, and *Science Books & Films*, and he is currently working on a memoir about teaching and science education.

About the Founding Editor

The late I. Edward Alcamo was a Distinguished Teaching Professor of Microbiology at the State University of New York at Farmingdale. Alcamo studied biology at Iona College in New York and earned his M.S. and Ph.D. degrees in microbiology at St. John's University, also in New York. He had taught at Farmingdale for over 30 years. In 2000, Alcamo won the Carski Award for Distinguished Teaching in Microbiology, the highest honor for microbiology teachers in the United States. He was a member of the American Society for Microbiology, the National Association of Biology Teachers, and the American Medical Writers Association. Alcamo authored numerous books on the subjects of microbiology, AIDS, and DNA technology as well as the award-winning textbook *Fundamentals of Microbiology*, now in its sixth edition.